The Best Of
OH! CANADIANS

Hysterically Historical Rhymes

Gordon Snell

with caricatures by

McArthur & Company

Toronto

Published in Canada in 2006 by
McArthur & Company
322 King St. West, Suite 402, Toronto, Ontario M5V 1J2
www.mcarthur-co.com
Text © 2006 by Gordon Snell
Cartoons © 2006 by Aislin

Library and Archives Canada Cataloguing in Publication

Snell, Gordon □   The best of Oh! Canadians / Gordon Snell and
                    Aislin.

ISBN 1-55278-607-2

1. Celebrities--Canada--Poetry. 2. Humorous poetry,
English.□3. Canadian wit and humor, Pictorial. I. Aislin II. Title.

PR6069.N44B47 2006   821'.914   C2006-903394-3

Cover illustrations by AISLIN
Layout, Design, and Electronic Imaging by MARY HUGHSON
Printed and bound in Canada by Webcom

The publisher would like to acknowledge the financial support of the
Government of Canada through the Book Publishing Industry Development
Program (BPIDP) and the Canada Council for our publishing activities.
The publisher further wishes to acknowledge the financial support of the
Ontario Arts Council for our publishing program.

10 9 8 7 6 5 4 3 2 1

McArthur & Company
Toronto

Canadians both young and old,
Flamboyant, fair, bizarre and bold,
From many worlds and many ages
Parade in triumph through these pages.
I give them all in dedication
To Maeve, my love and inspiration.

GS

This book is dedicated
to my love in Lachine.

A

The Best Of
OH! CANADIANS

Hysterically Historical Rhymes

Contents

Canada Goose / 13

Saint Brendan / 15

Leif Ericcson / 19

John Cabot / 21

Jacques Cartier / 24

Samuel de Champlain / 28

Henry Hudson / 32

Robert Cavelier de La Salle / 37

Sieur d'Iberville / 40

George Townshend / 46

James Wolfe / 49

James McGill / 53

George Vancouver / 57

Alexander Mackenzie / 61

Laura Secord / 67

Sir John Franklin / 71

William Lyon Mackenzie / 76

Sir John A. Macdonald / 81

Sir Sandford Fleming / 85

Timothy Eaton / 89

Louis Riel / 93

Alexander Graham Bell / 100

James Naismith / 104

Emily Carr / 107

Mackenzie King / 112

Lucy Maud Montgomery / 117

Robert Service / 121

Nellie McClung / 129

Lawren Harris / 132

Norman Bethune / 137

Frederick Banting / 141

Mary Pickford / 145

Billy Bishop / 150

John Diefenbaker / 154

Norma Shearer / 158

Winnie the Pooh / 163

Fay Wray / 166

Joseph-Armand Bombardier / 171

Pierre Trudeau / 175

René Lévesque / 182

Oscar Peterson / 186

Margaret Laurence / 191

Gordie Howe / 195

Maurice "The Rocket" Richard / 199

Tim Horton / 205

William Shatner / 209

Glenn Gould / 214

Norval Morrisseau / 218

The Dionne Quints / 222

Jean Chretien / 228

Leonard Cohen / 233

Donald Sutherland / 237

Paul Martin / 239

Brian Mulroney / 242

Joni Mitchell / 247

Gilles Villeneuve / 253

Dan Aykroyd / 255

Bret Hitman Hart / 259

Terry Fox / 262

Stephen Harper / 266

Wayne Gretzky / 268

Julie Payette / 273

Shania Twain / 275

Celine Dion / 277

Sasquatch / 281

THE CANADA GOOSE
(*Branta Canadensis*)

*(Canada Geese with their distinctive honking cry make a majestic sight as they
fly in huge numbers through the sky. But not everyone admires them:
some regard them as a messy nuisance and a threat, and seek to cull them,
while they also face danger from the guns of the hunter.)*

HONK, HONK!
Now let the heavens ring –
The Canada Geese are on the wing.
Behold us, making our migrations
In V for Victory formations.
HONK, HONK!
We voice our cry melodious –
Why do some humans find it odious?

BANG, BANG!
Cracks out the hunter's gun –
They want to kill us, just for fun,
And justify their cruel ballistics
With very dubious statistics.
BANG, BANG!
Our ways they may condemn –
But have we done more harm than them?

HONK, HONK!
My goslings, warmly nuzzling,
You'll find the world a little puzzling.
You'll grow up beautiful and proud
Then hear that sound so fierce and loud,
BANG, BANG!

Your life is soon cut short:
The human species call it sport.

HONK, HONK!
Like loons and beavers too
We are Canadians through and through –
And carrying our nation's name,
We fly with it to world-wide fame.
HONK, HONK!
Let Man come to his senses –
Befriending *Branta Canadensis*.

SAINT BRENDAN
(484 – 578)

Brendan was an Irish monk whose voyages to exotic lands were described
in a Latin narrative translated and circulated widely in Europe.
Many people believe his journeys took him as far as the American continent.

The Europeans who claim to be
The first, America to see —
Columbus, Cabot, Viking Leif —
May find their claims have come to grief.
There's one who says that First they ain't,
And he is Brendan, Sailor Saint.

That he was real, you can't debunk:
He was a holy Irish monk
Born fifteen centuries ago.
He founded monasteries, we know —
And from a Latin text we learn he
Made the most amazing journey.

Saint Brendan's voyage was designed
The Land of Promise for to find.
He'd dreamed of it, and had, they say,
Bizarre adventures on the way.

They saw upon one island's coasts
Birds that were really hordes of ghosts.
Towards a crystal tower they came,
Then to a mountain, belching flame,
An isle of giants, a curdled sea,
An isle with fruit on every tree;

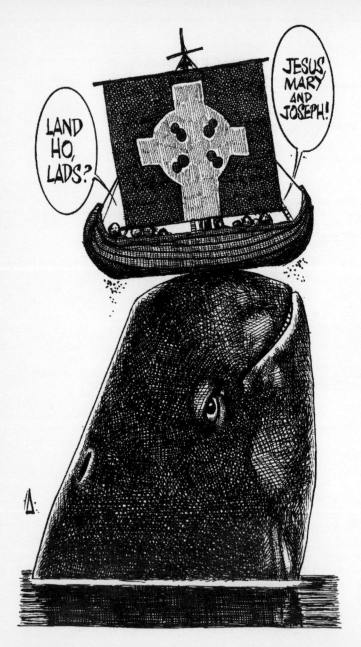

A rock where Judas had his station,
Let off, on Sundays, from Damnation.

And then they found the boat was beached:
Another isle they must have reached.
But soon the land began to rise:
It was a whale, of giant size.

The boat upon its back was stranded.
The Saint just said: "Well, since we've landed,
This chance we monks must not let pass:
We'll gather round, and say a Mass!"
And when the Mass was done, the whale
Sank down, and Brendan's ship set sail.

The tale's interpretation varies:
Some say he went to the Canaries,
To Iceland, and the Faroes too;
But others take a bolder view:
They say that Brendan's holy band
Went on as far as Newfoundland.

Tim Severin thought so, set afloat
A replica of Brendan's boat,
And though the weather was atrocious
The coast he reached was Nova Scotia's!

The day may come when we shall find
Some object Brendan left behind:
A Celtic cross, some rosary beads —
That sort of find is all it needs
To make all other claimants yield
And prove Saint Brendan led the field!

LEIF

LEIF ERICCSON
(died 1020)

According to the Viking sagas, Leif Ericcson crossed the Atlantic,
and the lands he visited are probably Baffin Island and Labrador,
and finally Vinland, which could be Newfoundland.

The average marauding Viking
Seized any land that took his liking.
No place was safe in early days
From Scandinavian forays.

Eric the Red first got a taste
To settle Greenland's icy waste,
And soon Leif Ericcson, his son,
His own great journeys had begun.

Over a thousand years ago
He was the first, the sagas show,
Who came from European lands
To step upon Canadian strands.
For those who watched those tall prows rise on
The empty, faraway horizon,
They must have made a curious sight
With spears and helmets gleaming bright.

To Baffin Island, where Leif came,
"The Land of Stones" he gave the name.
"The Wooded Land" he called the shore
Of what we know as Labrador.

In "Vinland" next that crew arrived,

And there the winter they survived.
They found there everything they wished:
Good pastures, salmon to be fished,
And even berries, grapes and vines —
That's why Leif called it "Land of Wines."

Though Vinland's written into history,
Its whereabouts is still a mystery.
Some choose Cape Cod, but others say
It's further north, near Hudson Bay;
And others claim they understand
It's on the coast of Newfoundland.

It must have been, if that is so,
Much warmer, centuries ago.
If only it had stayed that way,
We might be all enjoying today
The Newfoundlanders' Chardonnay.

But as it is, they've found their niche
With something stronger: pass the SCREECH!

JOHN CABOT
(1425 – c.1500)

*Originally from Italy, John Cabot went to England to get backing from
King Henry VII and the merchants of Bristol to search for a sea route to Asia.
He was the first of the explorers of that period to land
on the North American continent.*

For navigators, like John Cabot,
Ocean trips became a habit.
From youth, he heard the waters call —
He was Venetian, after all.

But Bristol merchants, and the King,
Financed John Cabot's journeying.
In 1497, he
Aboard the Matthew went to sea.
He reached the coast, we understand,
Most probably in Newfoundland.
In fact, the date he landed on
Was at the feast day of St John.

He raised a flag, in England's name,
Set several snares to capture game,
And said: "Lest anyone forgets,
I'll leave this needle too, for nets —
Then passers-by will be advised
This place is truly colonised."

No doubt the people living there
Were not aware, or didn't care
That he had come to their locality

And claimed to change their nationality!

More vital was the news he bore
Of oceans full of fish galore:
For Cabot on the way had found
The future Grand Banks fishing ground.

Though people praise Columbus more
For his trip, just five years before,
That sailor, after many dramas,
Had only got to the Bahamas;
While Cabot, with the same intent,
At least had reached the Continent.

Yet both explorers never ceased
To think that they had reached the East.
They didn't know, like us today,

America was in the way!

JACQUES CARTIER
(1491 – 1557)

*Jacques Cartier was the first European to explore the Gulf of St. Lawrence
and the St. Lawrence River. His encounters with the Iroquois ranged
from friendship to hostility, and the treasure he finally brought home
was not what he expected.*

"Sail west!" Jacques Cartier was told,
"And find me countries rich in gold."
The King of France had spoken, so
Jacques thought he'd really better go.
Besides, it was a mission which
With any luck, would make him rich.

He crossed the ocean, but he found
That Labrador was barren ground.
He treated it with some abhorrence —
But then he came to the St. Lawrence.
He crossed the Gulf, and made his way
Along the coast to Gaspé Bay.

And there he managed to annoy
The friendly local Iroquois
By putting up a giant cross
To show them all just who was Boss.

Chief Donnacona wasn't pleased —
But strained relations soon were eased.
It was Jacques' Gallic charm, we think —
Or was there something in the drink?
At any rate, Jacques took the chance

To ask the Chief's two sons to France.

The next year, when he brought them back,
They helped to put him on the track:
They showed him the St. Lawrence River.
"What riches I can now deliver!"
Exclaimed Jacques Cartier, as they told
Of distant kingdoms, full of gold.

He also thought the river went
Right through into the Orient.
And so, continuing his saga,
He sailed right on, to Hochelaga.

There, he was joyfully received.
He'd cure the sick, they all believed.
He read the Gospel of St John,
And though their pains and aches weren't gone,
They kindly didn't swear and curse:
At least, he hadn't made them worse.

A nearby mountain he did name,
And Mont-Royal it then became —
Now Montreal, the very same.
Then winter came, and scurvy too.
No Gospel cured that, Cartier knew.
The Iroquois' white-cedar brew
Was what saved most of Cartier's crew.

No thanks they got, but only grief:
In spring Jacques came and seized their Chief.
He took ten other prisoners too.

"I'll bring them back as good as new!"
That's what he promised, but we know
His vows all melted, with the snow.

To Canada the navigator
Did not return till six years later.
This time, he built a settlement:
To colonize was his intent.
But he was even more delighted
When gold and diamonds were sighted.

He thought that they'd be valued highly
And he would live the life of Riley.
But back in France, he found the ore
Was iron pyrites, nothing more,
And learned from valuers' reports
His diamonds were only quartz.

At least, the jewellers today
Have saved the name of CARTIER!

SAMUEL DE CHAMPLAIN
(1570-1635)

*Samuel de Champlain was an enthusiastic explorer
and map-maker who founded France's first colony in the
New World at Quebec in 1608.*

Champlain was eager to advance
His country's glory, in New France.
The best maps of the region then,
Came from his cartographic pen.
From Port-Royal, his earliest post,
He mapped the whole New England coast.

Explorers' trips, he realized,
Were best if locally advised.
So he made friendships, for insurance,
With the Algonquins and the Hurons.
When with these tribes his friendship grew
He travelled with them by canoe
And that was how he came to know
Lakes Huron and Ontario.
Then at another lake, said he:
"Let's call it Champlain, after me !"

Samuel was brave - among his stunts,
He shot the rapids, more than once.

Champlain was able to persuade
The French King that enormous trade
Would flow, if colonies were made.
He even thought it would be cute

When someone found the China route
To have on the Atlantic coast
A lucrative French Customs post.

After much thought, he chose the lands
Just in the place Quebec now stands.
His plans at first went topsy-turvy
When many settlers died of scurvy,
But Champlain never had a doubt:
He grew wheat, made a pool for trout,
And had a grand town plan laid out.

To make the winters seem less drear
He formed the Order of Good Cheer.
They'd hunt game for the festive table
And drink as much as they were able.

In transatlantic sailing ships
Champlain made over twenty trips,
And after one, he would decide:
"I'm forty - time I took a bride!"
The records, though, have never told
Just why he chose one, twelve years old.

Nor why, despite a happy life
In due course, with his grown-up wife,
He chose at last his will to vary
And leave all to the Virgin Mary.

He was exceedingly devout
And brought religious orders out
Among the tribes to make excursions
Attempting to promote conversions.

His colony survived a check -
The English capture of Quebec.
But then another deal was done:
Champlain was back, as Number One.
If thwarted, he cried: "Sacre Bleu! -
I'm here to act for Richelieu!"

He died, to solemn lamentation,
Where his first humble habitation
Had founded the Canadian nation.

HENRY HUDSON
(died 1611)

*Henry Hudson, who gave his name to so many places, made four voyages
searching for a northern route to the Pacific and China,
and was finally cast adrift in an open boat by his rebellious crew.*

Henry Hudson several times
Tried to sail to Eastern climes
Searching for the Isles of Spice,
But was always foiled by ice.

People thought the route northeast
Would lead to China at the least,
But up among the Arctic seas
Hudson found not one Chinese.

On the third trip, Hudson's men,
Ice-bound, grumbled: "Not again!"
A mutiny was in the air,
But Hudson fixed them with a glare:
"Well, if you feel like that," he said,
"We'll turn and sail northwest, instead!"
It made the sailors much less frantic,
Sailing over the Atlantic.

Up the Hudson River then
To Albany he took his men,
Thus showing that this waterway
Could be a trading route one day.
"Whatever this new land has got,"
Said Hudson, "China it is not!"

And so next year, in 1610,
Henry Hudson sailed again.
The spicy Orient was beckoning —
From the west, by Hudson's reckoning.

He believed that Davis Strait
Would be the Northwest Passage gate,
And lead him to an Arctic Sea
Which from drifting ice was free.
But the tide, so fierce and great,
Swept him to another Strait:
The one named Hudson, after him —
Though then, his fate was looking grim.

The crew began to rage and curse,
But turning round would just be worse.
Through icy seas they made their way
Four hundred miles, at ten per day,
Emerging into Hudson Bay.
Henry Hudson felt terrific:
He thought he'd entered the Pacific!

So south they sailed, and found James Bay,
Thinking that China lay that way.
Hudson searched for many days
But found the coast was like a maze.
And then there came the winter snows,
And all the land and waters froze.

Although they built a house on shore,
The winter chilled them to the core.
Now and then they caught some game,

But the dreaded scurvy came
And Henry Hudson got the blame.

When the ice broke up, they sailed:
Though the China trip had failed,
Hudson at the least could say
He'd discovered Hudson Bay.

But he never got the chance —
The others looked at him askance,
And what really roused their passions
Was finding Hudson's hidden rations.

After that, he got short shrift:
Rebels cast a boat adrift
With Hudson and eight men on board.
The rest cried: "That is your reward!"

A mystery surrounds the ends
Of Henry Hudson and his friends,
Left in the icy seas to float
In a leaky open boat.
Bligh kept such a group together,
But he had rather warmer weather!

Hudson, though, could not survive —
And yet his name remains alive:
The Bay, the Company, the Strait,
And towns and rivers, make him great.
But dying of cold and of starvation,
Great fame is not much consolation.

ROBERT CAVELIER DE LA SALLE
(1643-1687)

*La Salle crossed the Atlantic to New France with an ambition to explore
and to grow rich. He achieved these aims, but not entirely successfully,
since he both found - and lost - the Mississippi.*

La Salle, a would-be Jesuit,
After nine years was asked to quit.
Sulking, he said: "I'll take a chance
And try my fortune in New France."

A man devoid of inhibition,
He joined up with an expedition,
Telling the leaders: "I'm your boy,
For I speak fluent Iroquois."

His claim was shown to be absurd -
He couldn't understand a word.
But he declared: "I'll soon be back!"
And Governor General Frontenac
To whom he showed extreme servility
Promoted him to the nobility.

Back home in France, at Court he schemed
To clinch the deal of which he dreamed,
And soon two clerics with ambition
Helped get La Salle an expedition.
Then joyfully he shouted: "Yipee!
I'll sail right down the Mississippi!"

And so La Salle went sailing south
Right down the river to its mouth.

He then dressed up, so we are told,
In robes of scarlet and of gold
And stated: "I did everything
For Louis, France's glorious King.
He's now the Lord of this Nirvana -
Let's call the place LOUISIANA!"

The fur trade made his fortune grow;
His fort on Lake Ontario
And other ventures made La Salle
A V.I.P. in *Montréal*.

Then being a devious sort of chap
He showed the King a bogus map
Charting the Mississippi's flow
Far west of where it ought to go.
He told the King: "With this, it's true,
We'll conquer Mexico for you!"

He meant to land as he intended,
Just where the Mississippi ended;
But though he'd sailed it all before
He couldn't find it any more.
He told his party: "I'm afraid
The Mississippi's been mislaid!"

So up and down the coast they sailed
To seek the Delta, but they failed.
Sensing his men were in a tizz
La Salle said smoothly: "Here it is!"

They said: "This guy begins to vex us -

This, clearly, is the coast of Texas.
And we're so weary and sick of trying,
And while you're living, you'll go on lying -
Your Old Man River may disappear
But your own end is getting near.
Your fortunes now have reached rock bottom."
With that, they stood him up and shot him.

Considering La Salle's behaviour,
His claims to be their guide and saviour,
His grasping greed and his cupidity,
His treachery and sheer stupidity,
We all might wonder more and more
Just why he wasn't killed before!

SIEUR D'IBERVILLE
(1661 – 1706)

*(Canadian-born Sieur d'Iberville was one of the military
leaders whose many raids and battles by land and sea
established the colonies of New France. In the late 17th and
early 18th century these stretched from Hudson Bay south
as far as the Mississippi Delta.)*

When they settled in New France
Men of spirit got a chance
Their fame and fortune to advance.

One such was Charles le Moyne, who'd been
Brought here from France aged just fifteen,
A servant of the Jesuits;
With enterprise he used his wits
In trade and commerce, and he planned
Some profitable deals in land.
Among the rich in Montreal
He was the wealthiest of all.

Of his eleven sons, Pierre
In fierce forays would do and dare
To fight wherever it persists
The power of English colonists.

Pierre and his big brother Jacques
Led the Canadiens to attack
The village of Schenectady,
And there with ruthless savagery
They quite subdued the population,
Thanks largely to assassination.

Five times he led into the fray
A fighting force in Hudson Bay.
The English saw their first fort fall
When Pierre himself had scaled the wall;
Then d'Iberville and Jacques his brother
Saw one fort fall and then another.
With all the English chased away,
Sieur d'Iberville and France held sway
Over the whole of Hudson Bay.

Audaciously Pierre now planned
A fierce attack in Newfoundland.
He'd launch his daring raids upon
The stretch of land called Avalon.

From west to east his force would go
Across the wastes of ice and snow.
No other force from shore to shore
Had dared to go that way before.
Pierre's solution, though, was neat:
His men put snowshoes on their feet.

They travelled thus with some velocity
And then attacked with great ferocity.
The soldiers of Sieur d'Iberville
Two hundred settlers did kill,
And Pierre no doubt was overjoyed
To see a hundred boats destroyed.

"Angel of Wrath" the British called him –
We do not think the term appalled him.
As trophies of this grim attack

A load of scalps was soon sent back
To show to Governor Frontenac.

For all his furious rampages,
Pierre was certainly courageous.
He planned to take York Factory fort
But in thick fog he got caught short.
Sieur d'Iberville did not delay –
He sailed on into Hudson Bay,
Believing, though the light was dim,
His ships would soon catch up with him.

Then sure enough, the fog did clear
And soon he saw three masts appear.
Before a greeting left his lips
He realized they were English ships!

Their guns, when all was said and done,
Outnumbered his by three to one.
Although he was the lone defender
Sieur d'Iberville would not surrender.

He sailed towards his foes instead,
Guns blazing and full speed ahead.
The frigate fired – a cannon ball
Toppled his rigging, sails and all;
But firing promptly back at it,
He scored a devastating hit.

Two ships closed in – Pierre had seen them
And with a zig-zag sailed between them.
He could have fled and got away

And sailed out into Hudson Bay,
But then his foes he did astound:
Instead of fleeing, he turned around.

Once more an all-out war he waged –
For four fierce hours the battle raged
Until the frigate, out of luck,
Below the waterline was struck.

It quickly sank beneath the waves,
Taking the crew to watery graves.
Two other ships were lurking there
And one surrendered to Pierre.
The other, tiring of the fight,
Across the bay was taking flight.

His own ship sank – the crew survived;
And then at last the fleet arrived.
Pierre his plan would not forsake:
The fort he soon went on to take.

King Louis d'Iberville would thank
By giving him Chevalier rank
And saying: "Your style's so fast and nippy –
Run down and take the Mississippi!
And then extend our panorama
And take control of Alabama."

Now France's colonies held sway
From the Deep South to Hudson Bay –
A situation, many feel,
Helped hugely by Sieur d'Iberville.

Writers about him often feel
That "swashbuckling" was his appeal –
And when life put him to the test,
He swashed his buckle with the best.

GEORGE TOWNSHEND
(1724 – 1807)

(George Townshend came from an aristocratic family and joined the army as a young man. He was one of the three Brigadiers under General James Wolfe's command during the battle for Quebec in 1759. A talented artist, he drew caricatures of anyone he disliked in public or private life.)

In English eyes, George Townshend had
What really makes a guy count:
He was a wealthy, well-born lad
And Daddy was a Viscount!

So Wolfe, when Townshend joined his band,
Was not inclined to love him:
He felt that George was much too grand
And thought himself above him.

The General was a moody man
And somehow he'd arrange it
That every time he made a plan
He'd promptly go and change it.

The walls took quite a battering
While Wolfe planned his attack;
The Brigadiers were chattering
Behind their General's back.

While he was dithering about,
Oblivious to their strictures,
George got his pen and paper out
And started drawing pictures.

His fierce and expert artistry
Was savage and perfidious:
He made the General out to be
Deformed and crass and hideous.

His colleagues found the cartoons fun –
With laughter they were pealing;
But when the General spotted one
He nearly hit the ceiling.

The pair then had a raging row,
But George thought: "What the heck?
He can't do much about it now –
It's time to storm Quebec!"

The bullets flew, and on the ground
The stricken Wolfe lay bleeding –
And when he died, George Townshend found
That he himself was leading!

The French had battled for New France
And in the end had failed.
Now, when George Townshend got the chance,
For home he quickly sailed.

For fame and triumph George might thirst,
But he would surely soonest
Be honoured as the very first
Canadian cartoonist!

JAMES WOLFE
(1727 – 1759)

*James Wolfe reached the height of his military career in 1759 when he was
made commander of the British land forces in the expedition against the French
in Quebec. Though the attack succeeded, both he and the French general,
Montcalm, died in the battle.*

Wolfe started young — at just fourteen,
He first joined up as a Marine.
Perhaps it was coincidence
That out, of all the regiments,
The one that took him in was led
By James's father, at its head.

Marines for Infantry James swapped,
And then his progress never stopped.
He fought in Scotland, Belgium, France,
And then he got his biggest chance.

At Louisbourg he helped attack
The French ships, which were firing back;
He captured some, put some to flame,
And in that battle made his name.
Commander was his next position,
To take Quebec his army's mission.

The French defence force was Montcalm's:
Wolfe faced him without any qualms.
For James, in planning every fight,
Believed that he was always right —

50

A fact which often, it appears,
Caused quarrels with his Brigadiers.

Wolfe changed his plans throughout that summer:
Some were inspired, some rather dumber.
His main intention, though, was sound:
To tempt Montcalm to open ground.
But that sly General rightly thought:
"My fortress is a safer spot."

At last, and after several tries,
The British troops achieved surprise.
Boats full of soldiers, undetected,
Made landings where they weren't expected.
Beneath the cliffs, at dead of night,
They came ashore, and scaled the height.

Montcalm was now in quite a jam
There on the Plains of Abraham.
His enemy was growing stronger —
He knew that he could wait no longer.

So out he went; some progress made,
The French then met a fusillade.
The furious bombardment stunned them:
British forces had outgunned them.

Montcalm directed a retreat,
But never lived to see defeat:
A fatal bullet struck him down.
Wolfe never saw the captured town —
Although he reached the very portal,

The wounds that he received were mortal.
Quebec surrendered, but the war
Continued for a few years more.

The conquerors in this aggression
Were doubtful of their new possession.
So vast, so troublesome, so cold —
Was this a land they'd want to hold?
And some officials seemed to feel
To give it back had more appeal:
The French might think it quite a scoop
To swap the place for Guadeloupe...

And Canada, with that entente,
Would have une histoire différente!

JAMES McGILL
(1744 – 1813)

James McGill came from Scotland to join the fur trade in Canada.
He became a leading merchant and a civic figure in Montreal,
where he founded the university that bears his name.

Canada lured lots and lots
Of young and enterprising Scots,
And one from Glasgow felt the call
To come and live in Montreal.
His name is celebrated still:
He was the famous James McGill.

His University, begun
Way back in 1821,
Has nurtured many brilliant students
Of literature, and jurisprudence
For science, too, its classes cater —
In fact, no accolade is greater
Than saying: "McGill's my Alma Mater!"

Glasgow was where James went to college:
He had an early thirst for knowledge
And entered there, so we are told,
When he was only twelve years old.

At twenty-two, he'd emigrated —
In Montreal he was located;
And he was at the Great Lakes too
Dispatching parties by canoe
With voyageurs among the crew.

As more canoes like his departed
The northwest fur trade really started;
And in exchange for furs would come
Gunpowder, silver, cloth and rum.

Then as the fur trade grew and grew,
The canny merchants prospered too:
The warehouses on Rue Saint-Paul
Held James's wealth in Montreal.

When, angered by the Quebec Act,
America with troops attacked,
McGill and others made a pact
So Montreal would not be sacked.
Surrender was negotiated
And those invaders were placated.

Though Montreal was occupied,
James would not join the rebel side
And even voiced his detestation
Of this attempt at 'Liberation'.
To show McGill he was mistaken,
His cellar full of rum was taken.

When finally the armies went,
Benjamin Franklin then was sent
With revolutionary intent,
But found that none would heed his call
In French or English Montreal.
His journal, though, is with us yet:
It's called the Montreal Gazette.

The city prospered — James did too.
His civic reputation grew
And several times a seat he earned
When the Assembly was returned.
But he was not, for all his zest,
Deficient in self-interest.

In fact McGill was most adroit
Acquiring land around Detroit.
When that became a U.S. city,
He may have thought it was a pity,
But he obtained, by obligation,
Canadian lands in compensation.

That made him see it could be grand
To start to speculate in land.
Such enterprises made McGill,
Already wealthy, richer still,
And prompted him to make a will.

With gifts of money and of land
A University he planned,
Where many a future generation
Has owed to him their education;
And there Canadians honour still
The famous name of James McGill.

GEORGE VANCOUVER
(1757 – 1798)

George Vancouver's first voyages were with Captain Cook, but he is most celebrated for his epic four-and-a-half year journey along the western coast of Canada and the USA, charting over seventy thousand miles of coastline.

George Vancouver took a trip
At fourteen, on a naval ship.
His native England he forsook
To see the world with Captain Cook.
From him he was to learn the arts
Of making perfect maps and charts.

Cook's second trip with George aboard
The northwest coastal shores explored,
And George Vancouver was, what's more,
First European upon that shore.

Then off Cook went, two thousand miles,
To what he called the Sandwich Isles.
It's really hard to know just why he
Ignored their proper name, Hawaii.

The islanders thought Cook no friend,
And at their hands he met his end.
They nearly killed Vancouver too,
But he escaped with all his crew.

His death then would have been a pity —
For what would we have called the city?
But George lived on, and got promotion,

And sailed for the Pacific Ocean.
There, Spain was causing a commotion:
The coast was theirs, they had a notion.

The British government was furious,
Maintaining that the claim was spurious.
(The people living there, it's true,
Were never asked to give their view.)

Then José Martinez's band
Seized lots of British ships and land,
And when he dared to shout "Olé!"
The British cried: "No way, José!"

They needed now a speedy mover,
And so they sent in George Vancouver.
For what the British wanted most
Were surveys, up and down the coast.
"With those," they said, "you can declare
If there's a Northwest Passage there."

Some thought not all the coast was dry land —
Perhaps Alaska was an island?
George may have thought such views ridiculous,
But still, his survey was meticulous,
And all his skill and strength he put
Into that mapping, foot by foot.
The narrowest inlets he'd explore
In open boats, to reach the shore.

His survey, he could really boast,
Scanned sixty thousand miles of coast.

SKETCH by EMILY

HAT by TILLEY

EXPLORING by GEORGE

The small boats' trips increased the score
By something like ten thousand more.

Four years it took to bring it off —
Then, near the Isle of Baranof
Far to the north, Vancouver anchored
And took the rest for which he hankered.

"We've done it!" was his declaration,
"Get out the grog, in celebration!
And while we have our drinking session
Let's say farewell to one obsession,
The Northwest Passage! We have let it
Rule all our lives, and hope we met it.
Now we can simply say, 'FORGET IT!'
You might as well, to get to China,
Dig out a trench from Carolina."

Was he much wiser than he knew?
Digging a trench is what they'd do.
Southwards, years later, they installed it —
The Panama Canal they called it.

SIR ALEXANDER MACKENZIE
(1764 – 1820)

Alexander Mackenzie was ten when his family emigrated first to New York and then to Canada. He became a fur trader and made two epic journeys west, trekking by canoe and on foot in search of a route to the Pacific.

The search for furs; this was the quest
Which led Mackenzie to the west.
For there, the wilderness was rife
With every kind of furry life:
Beavers and otters, foxes, minks,
The wolf, the marten and the lynx.

They all made fashionable furs
And classy headgear, His and Hers.
For then the fur trade went unchecked,
Though not politically correct.
Creatures were killed without apology,
And no one cared about ecology.

The Athabasca River ran
Beside the new Fort Chipewyan,
And here Mackenzie's trek began.
With just twelve men in three canoes,
Slave River was the route he'd choose.
Off to the west they paddled forth,
Then found the river heading north.

Mackenzie wouldn't be downcast:
They paddled on, and paddled fast.
One hundred miles a day they went,

To reach the ocean their intent.
When finally they saw the sea,
All frozen it appeared to be.

Mackenzie grumbled: "What a shame!
This river here by which we came,
Let Disappointment be its name."
But others thought that name too grim,
And later named it after him.

His colleagues in the trade, however,
Were not impressed by his endeavour.
They said: "A sea of ice won't suit
As any kind of trading route."
Mackenzie though was resolute,
And four years later, with nine men
And one dog, he set out again.

Peace River was the way to go,
But did they find it peaceful? No!
Mackenzie and his nine companions
Faced rapids and cascades and canyons,
Hauled the canoe and all their goods
Up rocky paths through gloomy woods;
Midst snowy mountains, never warm,
They camped, and sheltered from a storm.

Mackenzie took the chance to write
Of all they'd done until that night,
Then in an empty rum keg placed
His diary of the route they'd traced
And all the dangers they had faced.

He cast the keg into the river
And hoped his note it would deliver.
The postal service now is better —
Then, it was chancier... and wetter!

For weeks Mackenzie and his team
Went bravely struggling upstream,
And wondered, was it all a dream?
Perhaps, although they'd done their best,
There was no river to the West.

But then they met a local guide
Who led them to the Great Divide.
And west from here, they had a notion,
Lay the great Pacific Ocean.
But soon, by icy waters battered,
Their lone canoe was nearly shattered:
Instead of paddling, as they planned,
They had to journey overland.

They found a river, guides who knew
This land where giant cedars grew,
And villages where they would dine
On salmon, deer, and porcupine.

But further on, the records tell us,
They met the warlike Bella Bellas
And found them much less friendly fellas.

An angry warrior climbed aboard
And grabbed Mackenzie's gun and sword,
And said white men, a few weeks back,

Had used such weapons to attack.
(The story that he told was true:
It was Vancouver and his crew.)

Back in his own canoe once more,
"Follow!" they heard the warrior roar.
Instead, they raced towards the shore;
They climbed a rock, and on the top
There for the night they had to stop.

Next day, as soon as it was light,
Two war canoes came into sight:
The outlook wasn't very bright.
And yet Mackenzie showed no fear —
He said: "Before we disappear,
The world must know that I was here!"

He wrote a record of his visit —
Like Kilroy, only more explicit:
Upon the rock, in letters great,
He scrawled his own name, and the date.
He wrote too, so they'd understand,
He'd come from Canada, by land.

The others neither groused nor brooded
To see their names were not included,
For they were more concerned that day
With how to make their getaway.

The warriors' canoes gave chase
But finally they lost the race;
Yet still Mackenzie had to face

The cruel journey back to base.
Somehow, the party made their way
At nearly forty miles a day,
And Alexander gained much glory
By later publishing his story.

Among the readers, for a start,
There was Napoleon Bonaparte:
He planned to beat the British back
With a Canadian attack.

Back home, the King did not demur,
But promptly dubbed Mackenzie "Sir".
Which shows what marvels can occur
From starting out to search for fur!

LAURA SECORD
(1775-1868)

*In the War of 1812, Laura Secord made an epic solo trek to warn the troops
at Beaver Dams of a coming attack. Public recognition and reward
were a long time coming, but she finally got her deserved fame,
as well as her name on monuments and chocolate boxes.*

In history, the name of Laura
Has come to have a certain aura,
Although it's true that no one now
Remembers what they called her cow.

In 1812 the Yankees, sore
At Canada, began a war.
The Secords, on the British side,
Found that their home was occupied.
The U.S. officers with pride,
Declaring they would soon be winners,
Told Laura she must cook their dinners.

What could she do? There in her house
She watched the officers carouse.
She listened too, as they began
To boast about their battle plan.
They said, "These troops of Uncle Sam's
Will wipe them out at Beaver Dams!"

So Laura thought, "I must give warning!"
Before the sun rose in the morning
She slipped away, quite undetected,
To say attack should be expected.

The day dawned and the hot sun shone
But Laura just walked on and on
Through undergrowth and hidden by-ways
Avoiding checkpoints, roads and highways.

She waded many a stream and river
Her urgent message to deliver,
And found her courage sorely tested
In treacherous swamps, by snakes infested.
And some accounts will tell you how
By clinging to a passing cow
She managed with this bovine aid
The soldiers' capture to evade.

She reached Niagara, and she paled:
How could that craggy cliff be scaled?
But Laura's courage never failed.
She climbed and clung and didn't stop
Until she'd reached the very top.

With darkness falling all around her,
A group of Mohawk warriors found her.
With wonder and concern they scanned her,
And brought her to the post's commander.

"Well, you deserve," said James FitzGibbon,
"A campaign medal and a ribbon.
I'll send the Mohawks on their track
And mount a great surprise attack!"

His victory hopes were not mistaken -
Five hundred prisoners were taken;
And everyone admired the way

That Laura Secord saved the day.

In spite of her courageous mission
Poor Laura got no recognition.
She sent out many a petition
In which she always chanced to mention
It would be nice to get a pension.

When more than forty years had passed
Her deed was recognized at last.
The Prince of Wales, the future King,
Just happened to be visiting
And made, among his many calls,
A visit to Niagara Falls.

Here it was brought to his attention
That Laura merited a pension.
He sent one hundred pounds all told;
Laura, now eighty-six years old,
Declared: "Well, better late than never!
At least my name will live for ever."

And when she died, her name was praised
And several monuments were raised.
In 1913, Frank O'Connor
Said, "Laura's name I'd like to honour.
She lived life well, and took the knocks -
I'll put her on my chocolate box!
Her portrait will be fine and dandy
Paraded on my luscious candy."

So Laura's name has never perished
Wherever chocolate is cherished.

SIR JOHN FRANKLIN
(1786 – 1847)

*John Franklin was a naval officer who charted thousands of miles
of Canada's Arctic coast in the quest for the Northwest Passage.
He made four expeditions and met his death during the last one.*

King William Island's frozen ground
Was where John Franklin's corpse was found,
His bones the only indication
Of that brave life of exploration.

From age fourteen, his naval life
Was filled with roving and with strife.
Then, Franklin saw his true vocation
In Canadian exploration.

The powers-that-be were all obsessed
With finding routes from east to west.
They sought the Northwest Passage which
Would help make everybody rich.

Franklin's first journey had no luck:
In polar ice they nearly stuck.
The second time from Hudson Bay
To Yellowknife he made his way,
Then down the river Coppermine —
The prospect, though, was far from fine.

Sometimes a frozen lake they crossed,
Their faces bitten by the frost.
Canoes on pairs of sleds were put:

Dogs dragged them, while men walked on foot.
The ice was honeycombed by rain,
And jagged edges caused great pain.
The men's and dogs' feet, when they bled,
Left on the ice a trail of red.

The journey seemed to take them ages,
And Franklin fumed with frequent rages.
No wonder that the Inuit feared
This sullen group, and disappeared.
And so, without the Inuits' aid,
The two canoes their journey made,
And for a month the coast surveyed.

Then food got short, and tempers too,
And murmurs of rebellion grew.
It wasn't long before John Franklin
Sensed grudges and resentments ranklin'.
He said: "We must return, it's plain:
I'll name this Point here Turnagain."
The men said: "Call it what you like —
But turn around, or we shall strike!"

They had no food, and their canoes
Were damaged far too much to use.
So overland the route they tried.
Frozen and starving, nine men died.
The rest, in order to survive,
Ate lichen just to keep alive.
A local tribe who knew the place
Found them, and brought them back to base.

Now, Franklin was a famous name;

The mysterious disappearance of Sir John Franklin finally explained...

And though a hero he became,
He found that life at home was boring,
And yearned again to go exploring.
Better equipped, he mapped once more
Hundreds of miles of Arctic shore.

Then late in life he got the chance
To make the final great advance.

Three hundred miles remained uncharted:
So for the Arctic coast he started —
But not before he watched them stowing
Three years' supplies to keep them going.
Steam boilers drove propellers, too,
And heated pipes to warm the crew.
A library of books was there,
And wine, cut-glass, and silverware.

In 1845, in May,
The ships sailed out to Baffin Bay.
But no one knew what happened then
To Franklin and his ships and men.
In that white world, so wild and weird,
They had completely disappeared.

The years passed — forty expeditions
Went sailing out on searching missions.
And Franklin's widow did her best
To press for yet another quest.
When she had waited fourteen years,
A gruesome find confirmed her fears.

King William Island was the site
Where Franklin's body came to light:
Two skeletons, one his, they guessed
From silver spoons that bore his crest.

The Northwest Passage now was mapped,
And in its icy wastes were trapped
Many explorers' ships and crews
Whose families had received no news
Of how they suffered and they died,
Unknown and unidentified.

At least they found John Franklin's grave —
A stern explorer, rash and brave:
For charts and maps his life he gave.

Though Europeans' success was heady,
The Inuit knew that coast already;
If Franklin with his dedication
Had sought out their co-operation,
He might have saved the situation.

WILLIAM LYON MACKENZIE
(1795 – 1861)

*A journalist and a politician, Mackenzie was a tireless and fierce advocate of
reform. As a member of Upper Canada's Assembly, he was expelled
and re-elected many times, and became the first mayor of Toronto.
In 1837 he led an unsuccessful rebellion, fled to the U.S.A,, was jailed, and then
returned after an amnesty to further turbulent years in Canadian politics.*

The mind of William Lyon Mackenzie
Was in a state of constant frenzy.
When Tory values were the norm,
He preached political reform.

He started, to promote his aims,
Papers with many different names.
When one would fail, he wasn't vexed:
He'd bounce right back and start the next.

In Upper Canada's Assembly
Mackenzie's foes were all a-trembly.
He lashed the opposition ranks
And even criticised the Banks —
An attitude, which some might say,
Would also find support today...

He was elected, then rejected,
And then once more was re-elected.
In such esteem the people held him
That when his enemies expelled him
A crowd of several hundred went
And marched right into Parliament.

And after that the by-election
Made him the popular selection.

Then Yonge Street rang with cheers of praise,
As bagpipes and a hundred sleighs
Went in a great procession, led
By William, riding at the head.

Yet still his foes, infuriated,
Kept booting out the man they hated —
But he was always re-instated.
He said: "If this goes on much more,
I'll ask for a revolving door!"

Now when Toronto first was founded,
Up to new heights Mackenzie bounded.
The brand new Council then and there
Made William Lyon Mackenzie mayor.
But in provincial politics
He couldn't beat the Governor's tricks:
That ruling agent of the Crown
Kept putting the reformers down.

Mackenzie now began devising
A plan to stage an armed uprising.
He wrote, to fuel the demonstration,
An Independence Declaration,
And made, to gather his supporters,
Montgomery's Tavern his headquarters.
They prepared to sally forth, "Best
Take Toronto from the west."

Thursday was meant to be the day
When they would all be on their way,
But someone gave the city warning
And so they marched on Tuesday morning.
Then by the Guards with bullets spattered,
Mackenzie's rebel army scattered.

Though further reinforcements then
Came to increase Mackenzie's men,
The city's soldiers came to meet them
And swiftly managed to defeat them.

Mackenzie fled, the battle lost —
Niagara's River then he crossed,
And soon on Navy Island there
Americans arrived to share
As volunteers, with his persuasion,
A plan for Canada's invasion.

They were bombarded from the bank
And then their main supply ship sank,
And soon the U.S. Government
Decided it was time they went.

For William, prosecution waited:
Neutrality he'd violated.
Released on bail, not beaten yet,
He started up a new Gazette,
And wrote, with somewhat rash intent,
Attacks upon the President.

Jailed for a year, he then was pardoned,
And soon his attitudes had hardened.
Back home in Canada once more,
A lot of things made William sore.
He lashed old colleagues, and old laws —
A rebel upon every cause.
He was a man of great panache,
Eccentric, maverick and rash.

Our parties might have more appeal
With some of his reforming zeal.

SIR JOHN A. MACDONALD
(1815 – 1891)

John Macdonald began his career as a lawyer in Kingston, Ontario,
then entered politics, becoming the leader of the Conservatives and in 1867
the first Prime Minister of the new federal Canadian nation.

John was, at twenty-one, a star –
The judges called him to the Bar.

Though soon, by some opponents' reckoning,
Bars of another kind were beckoning,
John thrived in party politics
And quickly mastered all the tricks.
Premier by 1856,
He saw that only Federation
Could forge a new Canadian nation.

So in Quebec the delegations
Began, some with persistent patience,
Others with fiery protestations,
To try to find a joint solution
And hammer out a constitution.

Eighteen days talking it would need
To get the document agreed.
So after many a deal, and dance,
Confederation got its chance.

It finally became a fact
When Britain opted to enact
The British North American Act.

Then politicians must debate
How to describe this latest state.
A Kingdom? Oh dear, no – because
A Kingdom's just what Britian was.

New Brunswick Premier Leonard Tilley
Believed such nit-picking was silly.
He said: "The Psalms, in my opinion,
Suggest we use the name Dominion,
For one of them declares that "He
Dominion shall have from sea to sea."

They all agreed upon the name;
John A. Macdonald then became
The first Prime Minister to stand
As leader of this great new land.

He did indeed think it should be
A land that stretched from sea to sea,
And so, to realize the dream
He backed a most audacious scheme
To build a grandiose creation;
A Railroad that would span the nation.

He thought that, as in all his deals,
Some patronage would oil the wheels.
Hugh Allen and his syndicate
Would think a railroad contract great
And Allen made most generous offers
To swell Macdonald's party coffers.

The syndicate would be selected
When John Macdonald was elected –
But there was something he neglected:
Surprise, surprise – he never thought
To tell the people he'd been bought!

But soon the Liberals told the world
And what a scandal then unfurled.
His reputation undermined,
Sir John reluctantly resigned.

But five years later, he was back –
The railroad plan was back on track.
This stunning engineering feat
In only four years was complete.

And soon it carried troops to quell
The second rising of Riel.
Macdonald chose a rash solution
And authorized his execution.
The anger and recrimination
Threatened once more to split the nation.

Somehow the Grand Old Man survived
And in the next election thrived.
He died, still in the driving seat,
His colourful career complete.
He had well earned his reputation
As Father of Confederation.

SIR SANDFORD FLEMING
(1827 – 1915)

*As a railway engineer, Sandford Fleming helped to build
the new railroads across Canada. He invented the international system
of Time Zones still used today.*

Many good results are stemming
From the work of Sandford Fleming:
Railways, time zones, maps and charts,
Aid for science and the arts,
Progress all across the land
Was helped by Fleming's guiding hand.

An engineer and a surveyor,
He soon became a major player
Among the ranks of those who pressed
For a railroad east to west.

In Newfoundland, and on the plains,
He planned the tracks to take the trains.
Up in the Rockies fierce disputes
Flared up about the likely routes,
But Fleming was a pioneer
Who liked to get his way, it's clear —
And, well — he was Chief Engineer!

Soon, trains across the land would hurry —
But Sandford Fleming had a worry.
He'd rush to catch a train, and miss it,
And curse in language most explicit;

With rage he made his protests vocal:
"The time we keep is too damned local!"

For way back then, each township said:
"At noon, the sun's straight overhead."
So when Quebec said: "It's noon, pronto!"
"Eleven-thirty!" said Toronto.
This caused rail travellers some vexation,
Changing their watches at each station.

So Fleming then said: "How sublime
If we could have a Standard Time.
A twenty-four hour clock we need,
Which even idiots can read.
The world we should divide, what's more,
In Time Zones, making twenty-four.
On every clock, one time is shown
Until you reach another zone."

Both here and in the U.S.A.
The railway managers said: "Hey!
We do believe you've shown the way."

But others said that Fleming's scheme
Was just another crackpot's dream;
And some declared his plans so flighty
They even flouted God Almighty.
These zealots never stopped condemning
The sinful ways of Sandford Fleming.

It took some years of arguments
Till scientists and governments
Agreed that Fleming's plan made sense.

In 1884 they opted
For Standard Time to be adopted.
So Fleming was triumphant then —
And never missed a train again.

That wasn't all, by any means:
He was the Chancellor of Queen's,
And back in 1851,
When postage stamps were first begun,
He drew the first Canadian one.

He helped to make Canadians able
To reach Australia by cable,
And when he'd nothing else to do
He even wrote a prayer book too.

No wonder people were delighted
When he, aged seventy, was knighted.
Perhaps when honoured by the Queen
She asked the time, and he was seen
To say: "Which Time Zone do you mean?"

A nod to Fleming is a must
For travellers, however fussed,
Each time their watches they adjust.

TIMOTHY EATON
(1834-1907)

*Timothy Eaton founded the first of the Eaton chain of stores in Toronto in 1869,
and his commercial ideas revolutionized shopping in Canada.*

From Ireland to Canadian shores
To found a famous chain of stores
Came Timothy Eaton, now renowned
Wherever shoppers can be found.

Shopping was ripe for revolution
On Eaton had his own solution;
And so in 1869
The first store in the Eaton line
At Yonge Street started operation
And caused at once a big sensation.

Eaton began with great panache,
Declaring: "We take only cash.
The barter system, we have shed it -
What's more, you needn't ask for credit,
Because you just ain't gonna geddit!

Don't seek to bargain, for we won't -
You pay our fixed price, or you don't.
We offer value and fair play -
That's retailing, the Eaton way!"

But one more promise Eaton made
Really amazed the retail trade:
He said, "We'll give back what you paid

EATON

If you are not quite satisfied
With any product we supplied."

His rivals scoffed, and said disaster
Would come within a year, or faster.
But Timothy soon proved them wrong
As shoppers to his store did throng.

And what was even more surprising,
He wanted honest advertising -
Insisting, "Everything must be
Exactly what we guarantee.
No lies and no exaggeration
Must mar the Eaton reputation."

He made more innovations later -
Even installed an elevator.
When customers at first were wary
He tried to show it wasn't scary:
Wax figures then were put inside
And up and down were seen to ride -
A ruse that was a bit surprising
From one who liked true advertising.

Now as the Eaton empire grew
He pioneered mail-order too.
His catalogue was justly famed:
The Prairie Bible it was named.

While Eaton's name grew more prestigious
The founder still remained religious.
He hated liquor, wouldn't let

His stores sell any cigarette.
At home, nobody had the chance
To play a game of cards, or dance.

At work, he was paternalist -
A fervent anti-unionist.
His workers even were afraid
To watch the Labour Day parade.

And yet, unlike the rest, he'd fix
For Eaton's stores to close at six;
And afternoons on Saturday
He said should be a holiday.

His methods prospered - soon he'd boast
A chain of stores from coast to coast.
Then, with the founding father gone,
His sons and grandsons carried on.

LOUIS RIEL
(1844-1885)

*Louis Riel led two rebellions trying to establish lands and rights for the Métis,
descendants of indigenous peoples and early European settlers. His campaigns
both peaceful and military, led to the founding of Manitoba, but his eventual
trial and execution caused long-lasting and passionate controversy.*

The Métis, from two races grown,
Became a nation of their own.
To the Red River thousands went
And made a farming settlement,
And twice a year they all would go
To hunt the herds of buffalo.

This bright boy from the distant prairie
Went eastward to a seminary.
In Montreal his education
Earned him a dazzling reputation.
Mastering Math, French, Greek and Latin,
Louis topped every class he sat in.

And while the boy was educated
Four provinces were federated
To make what was, in their opinion,
A most spectacular Dominion.

Sir John Macdonald was Prime Minister.
The Métis didn't think him sinister;
But Canada approached one day
The Company called Hudson's Bay
And told them the Dominion planned

To buy out most of 'Rupert's Land'.
They said, "We fear a confrontation
Will lead to US annexation
Unless it's checked by our new nation."

Although the land was bought and sold
The people living there weren't told.
So when they saw surveyors there
Rebellion was in the air.
Louis, their chosen leader, went
To ask what these intruders meant.
"You have no rights here," said Riel.
(The less polite said, "Go to hell!")

The land surveyors then withdrew -
So did Macdonald's Governor too.
Fort Garry was the new H.Q.
And over it a new flag flew -
The Métis flag for all to see,
Resplendent with the fleur de lis.

Riel proclaimed a government
And was elected President.
Macdonald sent out Donald Smith
For Louis' men to parley with:
His promises were just a myth.
The Métis, thinking they were meant,
Believed that Canada's intent
Was totally benevolent.

And so they set their prisoners free,
But they abused their liberty.

95

Each called himself a Canada Firster:
As racists, there was no one worster.
They marched in fury on Fort Garry
But snowdrifts forced the troops to tarry
And so the expedition failed:
They were surrounded, caught and jailed.

Perhaps unwisely then, Riel
Called on their leader in his cell.
He was a man called Thomas Scott,
The angriest bigot of the lot.

He threatened he would kill Riel -
He beat the warder up as well.
For bearing arms against the state
Scott went on trial and learned his fate:
By firing squad his end he'd make.
It proved to be a big mistake:
Scott's standing up to then was zero,
But now he was Ontario's hero.

Macdonald wished the Métis nation
To join the growing Federation
So with a Métis delegation
He did a deal for integration.

Riel's dream province was a fact
Under the Manitoba Act.
Riel rejoiced, but in the end
Found John Macdonald was no friend.

The velvet glove, he'd understand,

Concealed a ruthless iron hand.
The force that claimed it came to police
Would never give the rebels peace.

And so Riel was forced to roam,
An exile from his own true home.
And though three times his people sent
Riel to sit in Parliament
The Government despite this call
Would not admit him there at all.
At last, "You're pardoned," they would say,
"Provided that you stay away."

The Métis, overwhelmed and fleeced
By settlers coming from the east,
By now had in large numbers gone
To live by the Saskatchewan.
From tribal ancestors they came,
And felt the land was theirs to claim.

Though Ottawa at length agreed,
It acted with such lack of speed
The Métis knew they must rebel -
And who could lead them but Riel?

And Louis welcomed the decision -
He had a messianic vision
That he was chosen now to be
The man to make his people free.

With meetings and a Bill of Rights
He tried to do it with no fights.

But secret forces then were sent
By John Macdonald's government
Which feared the Métis, wanting more,
Would spark a greater Civil War.

Only two Cree lent their might
To give support to Louis' fight.
And yet he found that he could meet
The soldiers, and inflict defeat.

Louis Riel's success in arms
Set off a series of alarms -
Macdonald said in some despair:
"We need to get troops quickly there."

The railroad's chief said, "We will chance it
If you in turn will just finance it!"
So, soon the railroad's gaps were filled,
The troops sent, many Métis killed -
Reduced, when ammunition fails,
To firing buttons, stones and nails.

The troops could no more be defied:
Riel surrendered and was tried.
He told the jury that his aim
Had always only been to claim
The land rights in his people's name:
But then the Guilty verdict came.

The jury made a plea for mercy:
The Crown, ignoring controversy,
Hanged Louis - and by that ensured

A quarrel that has still endured.
Rebel or martyr? Though he's gone,
The argument still carries on.

Riel declared it made him sick
That Protestant and Catholic
Could not shake hands - he voiced his fears
That this could take two hundred years.

Progress has since been somewhat slow -
Still, there's a century to go!

ALEXANDER GRAHAM BELL
(1847 – 1922)

*Bell was born in Scotland and moved to Canada with his parents in 1870.
His lifelong interest was teaching the deaf to speak, but he was a brilliant
inventor: a pioneer not only of the telephone, but of sound recording,
sonar detection, hydrofoils, and flying machines.*

Alexander Graham Bell,
His parents thought, was far from well.
So they decided they would go
To Brantford, in Ontario..
Once there, his health improved immensely,
And he began to work intensely.

Enthusiastically he'd teach
His father's system, Visible Speech.
The symbols, which were quite unique,
Could help the deaf to learn to speak.

And meanwhile Bell pursued with zest
Another scientific quest.
For it was one of his desires
To send speech by electric wires.
Thus he believed we could, one day,
Converse with people far away.

The telephone was in the offing —
Which didn't stop the people scoffing.
To make words carry, they'd no doubt
The only thing to do was shout!
And when they heard what Bell was after,
They simply doubled up with laughter.

101

But Bell and Watson, his assistant,
Remained courageous and persistent,
And in their workshop day and night
They toiled to prove that they were right.

 Watson one night heard Bell's voice call —
It wasn't coming through the wall,
But down the wires, to Watson's ear:
"Please come here, Watson!" loud and clear.
Watson rushed in to tell his mentor:
"You sure are one great inventor!"

Bell got his patent applications
For his "electric undulations",
And very soon he got the chance
To make a really great advance.

From Tutela Heights his voice would go
To Paris, in Ontario.
And later, when he made a call
To greet his friends in Montreal,
They all cried, when they heard him speak:
"Le Téléphone — c'est magnifique!"

But then, big telegraphic firms
Boldly infringed the patent's terms;
To back his claim, Bell did resort
To lengthy battles through the court.

His company, Bell Telephone,
Was internationally known,
But Bell's resolve was unrelenting:
He just went on and on inventing.

He sent sound down a beam of light
And made experiments with flight,
Like an enormous man-powered kite;
And as these craft got off the ground,
Bell pioneered recorded sound.

Today, he would approve when shown
The wonders of the mobile phone —
But would he really wish to toast
The chatty radio phone-in host?

Or would he feel that each invention
Has some effects too brash to mention?
Such outcomes he could hardly know
Of that first call, so long ago,
At Brantford, in Ontario.

JAMES NAISMITH
(1861-1939)

*James Naismith, from Almonte, Ontario, gained a doctorate in
theology in Montreal, He became a gymnastics teacher and inspired
his students by inventing the modern game of basketball.*

James Naismith studied at McGill:
Theology was his great skill.

But then, instead of being a preacher,
He worked as a gymnastics teacher.
And in that role, in Springfield, Mass.,
His greatest triumph came to pass.
There clever James amazed them all
When he invented basketball.

Lessons in his gymnasium
Had left his students feeling glum:
Some new game he must now devise
To make them want to exercise.

The janitor he then beseeches:
"Those baskets there, which carry peaches —
Please get me two of them, my friend,
And nail them up, at either end.
And when they're hanging on the wall
Then bring me, please, a soccer ball."

The janitor knew his propensity
For doing things with mad intensity —

And so he did what James requested
And soon this brand-new game was tested.

Although the students cried: "What fun!"
The score was only Nought to One.
They soon improved upon that figure,
And with each game the scores grew bigger.

This didn't please the janitor,
For after each and every score
The ball was trapped — he couldn't leave it,
But had to climb up and retrieve it.
He chuckled when the players fumbled,
But every time they scored, he grumbled.

He said: "Why was this game invented?
Those baskets have me quite demented.
I'm sorry now I ever got 'em:
Why don't I just cut off the bottom?"
He did, and Naismith with a whoop
Cried: "Great! Let's call the thing a hoop!"

The sport took off, and grew in fame —
But still it hadn't got a name.
The students said: "What we must do
Is call this new game after you. "

But James, being modest, thought it plain
That that would be a little vain.
It's just as well, for after all,
Who'd play a game called NAISMITHBALL?

EMILY CARR
(1871-1945)

*Emily Carr, one of Canada's greatest and most original painters,
had to wait till she was fifty before her art got any wide recognition.
She grew up in Victoria, not the ideal setting for her eccentric and volatile
personality. But her great joy was travelling among the distant forest
and coastal communities of British Columbia, whose lifestyle
and totem pole art she recorded in her work.*

The Old World painters were inclined
To think that Art should be refined.
Canada's landscape they pooh-poohed:
"Those vistas are too vast and crude -
Unpaintable, that's what they are!"
But then, along came Emily Carr.

Her early sketches go right back
To charcoal portraits, on a sack.
Another childhood interest grew
In cherishing wild creatures too.
She tamed a squirrel and a crow -
And played guitar, and learned to sew.

In that strict family of nine
She was most often out of line,
And she remained throughout her life
A rebel who attracted strife.

Into the forest she would roam,
The local people's ancient home;
And so began her fascination
For many a centuries-old First Nation.

Some of the early friends she made
Lived near a Mission where she stayed.
Liking her warmth and sense of fun
They called her Klee Wyck - 'Laughing One'.
(The Mission, treated with aversion
By contrast, made just one conversion.)

In England then she studied art;
A suitor who had lost his heart
Followed her there across the sea
And kept on asking, "Marry me!"

This happened several times a week,
And she'd refuse each time he'd speak.
In fact, though several suitors tried,
She never did become a bride.

Back home, Victoria's ways she mocked:
Her sisters were extremely shocked.
She smoked, her words were sometimes coarse -
She even rode astride a horse!

Vancouver made a change of scene:
There, happier than she'd ever been,
She taught enthusiastically
Surrounded by her 'family' -
A dog, raccoons, a cockatoo,
Squirrels and chipmunks formed the crew.
Students, in spite of all these creatures,
Found Emily the best of teachers.

The places that she loved the most
Were in the woods and on the coast.

She got to know the vital roles
Played by the huge, carved totem poles.
She painted pictures of them, fearing
This art would soon be disappearing.

On Emily's journeys with her tent
A small menagerie always went.
The dog and cockatoo both came -
Even a vulture she'd made tame.

The villages and woods inspired her
And then a trip to Paris fired her:
She saw, instead of old precision,
A new art with a big, bold vision.
Now Emily with this art acquainted,
Knew how her landscape could be painted.

But back at home, her striking style
Provoked a condescending smile.
They called the work of Emily Carr
Childish and clumsy and bizarre.
Her sister, blind to Emily's aims,
Told her, "I simply love the frames!"

She kept on painting, loving best
The coast and forests of the West.
Their people's outlook she could share,
And found her firmest friendships there.

But even artists have to eat,
And Emily, to make ends meet,
Ran an apartment house, although
The dining-room made quite a show -

It doubled as a studio.
She felt this life was like a penance
And used to fight with all the tenants.

No fame or fanfares Emily knew
Till she was over fifty-two.
The National Gallery played a part:
It staged a show of West Coast Art.
At that exciting exhibition
Her art at last got recognition.

She'd been praised long ago in Paris:
Now she delighted Lawren Harris.
Soon she attained artistic heaven -
A show among the Group of Seven.
In Lawren Harris she had found
A mentor, fiery and profound.

He bought her paintings and declared:
"This Western genius must be shared.
If for a masterpiece you search,
Here's Emily's painting, Indian Church".

So Emily Carr at last became
In art a celebrated name;
And when she reached her seventieth year
Began a literary career.

Her stories brought her instant fame:
The first book's title was the same
As that fine nickname she had won -
Klee Wyck, which means The Laughing One.

WILLIAM LYON MACKENZIE KING
(1874 – 1950)

*(King was the grandson of the 1837 rebel leader, William Lyon Mackenzie,
but had a much more cautious personality. First elected as a Liberal
to the House of Commons in 1908, he became Canada's longest reigning
Prime Minister, winning six elections and pursuing sometimes contradictory
policies. He led a united Canada through the Second World War
and the boom years that followed it.)*

William Lyon Mackenzie King
Clung to his mother's apron string –
And his Mamma was far from critical
When William chose to get political:
If politics absorbed his life
He really didn't need a wife!

In Parliament he made his name –
The Liberals' leader he became.
King, welcomed with admiring cheers,
Led them for nearly thirty years.

Into the fray he boldly bounced –
Meighen's Conservatives were trounced.
For years King led a coalition
While Meighen fumed in opposition.

Then King's support began to waver;
A bold solution he would favour:
The Governor General, he'd declare,
Should call elections then and there.
"I won't!" Lord Byng, the G.G., said.
"Meighen shall govern in your stead."

Three days of power Meighen tasted;
The Governor General was lambasted
By furious Mackenzie King:
"A devious meddler, that's Lord Byng!
He's trying to play colonial tricks
With our Canadian politics!"

Whether King's view was right or wrong,
Most of the voters went along:
The Governor General, they said,
Should henceforth be a figurehead.
Though Byng might grumble, grouse and glower,
Mackenzie King was back in power.

And now he started to create
The groundwork for a welfare state.
(Not for First Nations – they would note
Their chance of justice was remote:
They didn't even get to vote.)

King's style was full of incongruity –
He liked strategic ambiguity.
Elusive, cunning, enigmatic,
And brilliantly bureaucratic,
He seemed to move, while staying static.

In séances he sometimes tried
Communing with The Other Side,
And asked dead leaders if they knew
What policies he should pursue;
He tried to reach his mother, too.

114

King joined the War, but said: "It's clear
We're having no conscription here."
Instead, he sent each volunteer
Who'd signed up for defence alone
Abroad into the battle zone.

Conscription came – though many grieved
That somehow they had been deceived.
Mackenzie King just dodged and weaved,
And got his moral stance believed.

At home, his policies were hard:
Most Jewish refugees were barred,
And Japanese Canadians found
For "relocation" they were bound.

King made such harsh rules with impunity,
And still maintained Canadian unity.
After the war, he let the nation
Reluctantly, take immigration,
But made the rules as he thought right,
To favour those whose skin was white.

And yet, King helped to lay foundations
That started the United Nations,
And turned, with diplomatic stealth,
An Empire to a Commonwealth.

His final stature's still a mystery –
Perhaps the verdict of our history
Will always have a lingering doubt:
Years later, still the jury's out.

Just as he sought for a result
By dabbling with things occult,
Perhaps in rooms discreet and dim
Our leaders are consulting him!

LUCY MAUD MONTGOMERY
(1874 – 1942)

The author of the celebrated children's book, "Anne of Green Gables",
was born on Prince Edward Island, where the book is set. She grew up there
with her grandparents, and only left when she married in 1911 and
moved to Ontario, where she continued to write more "Anne" stories.

At four years old, in church one day,
Maud asked her aunt where Heaven lay.
She pointed upwards — Maud, ecstatic,
Assumed that it was in the attic.
In future, in whatever station,
She was less sure of its location.

She felt, when she was only nine,
That literature should be her line.
A blank verse poem she began;
Her father, not a tactful man,
Read it and said, as Maud's heart sank,
"You're right, my dear, it's very blank!"

Prince Edward Island was their home,
Although Maud's father liked to roam,
And several businesses did spawn
Way over in Saskatchewan.

His wife had died when Maud was two,
And so with grandparents she grew,
Upon a farm in Cavendish —
As fine a place as she could wish.
Its beauties, rural and inviting,
Were later to inspire her writing.

Grown up, she taught, and also wrote —
At 6 a.m., wrapped in a coat.
Her first paid work was to be seen
By readers of a magazine:
Verses for which her recompense
Was garden seeds, worth fifty cents.

A newspaper in Halifax
Gave her a job like any hack's:
Society columns, Tea-Time Chat,
Which she was very skilful at.
But all the time she was aspirin'
To be another Keats or Byron.

And then she wrote a novel which,
To her amazement, struck it rich.
Anne of Green Gables was the name
That launched her into wealth and fame.
It told how Anne the orphan came
To join the Cuthberts, at eleven,
And found Prince Edward Island heaven.

Anne's chattering ways, her wild elation,
Her passionate imagination,
Her eager schemes, her tough resilience,
Would bring her readers by the millions.

Though some reviewers made Maud sore —
(The New York Times called "Anne" a bore) —
The rest were most enthusiastic,
And Mark Twain thought the book fantastic.

Then a new life for Maud began,
With marriage to a clergyman.
She was a mother and a wife
And lived a calm, church-centred life.
Although she did it very well
She missed Prince Edward Island's spell,
And visits there would always be
A journey into memory.

Meanwhile, her readers all desired
More of the girl they so admired.
Anne of Green Gables was adored:
"Give us more stories!" they implored.

These Maud Montgomery supplied,
Though wearily she sometimes sighed:
"I wish that I could turn the tables,
And close the shutters on Green Gables!"

But still more fame would come her way:
There were two movies, and a play —
Yet Anne's creator got no pay.
Her contract, though she reached the heights,
Had never mentioned movie rights!

And now, though Maud herself is gone,
Her sparky heroine lives on,
And visitors from many lands
See where the house Green Gables stands.

And maybe, since she took the view
Reincarnation could be true,
Does Maud Montgomery see it too?

ROBERT W. SERVICE
– and those who came after him...
(1874 – 1958)

Robert Service's boisterous ballads about characters like Dangerous Dan McGrew earned him huge popularity as the Bard of the Yukon. He arrived from Scotland as a young man, and after years of roving he became a bank clerk in Whitehorse and Dawson City soon after the great Gold Rush days.

The life of Robert W. Service
Would make most normal people nervous.
His journeys through the frozen wastes
Were not to everybody's tastes —
But though in life they'd do without them,
They simply loved to read about them,
And with his books he was, henceforth,
The Bard of the Canadian North.

Brought up in Scotland, as a lad
A taste for verse he always had,
And on his poetry he'd work,
When in the bank he was a clerk.
When done with debtors and with creditors,
He'd send his poems off to editors,
Who published his poetic flights
In People's Friend and Scottish Nights.

Then of the banking life he tired:
By wanderlust he was inspired.
Young Robert said he couldn't wait
To board a ship and emigrate.
With joy he stood upon the deck

To watch the docking at Quebec.
He had a ticket to the west
And just five dollars in his vest.

The crowded train moved down the track —
He slept upon the luggage rack;
And on that journey he was quite
A striking, if a curious, sight.
For he was dressed like Buffalo Bill:
His feet high circus-boots did fill,
And on his head, so debonair-o,
He wore a dashing black sombrero.

Fine, if in movies he'd appeared —
In Winnipeg he just looked weird.

But as the train went on and on
Most of his gear was quickly gone.
He had to sell things, one by one:
His suit, his camera, his gun.

Yet on the Rockies as he gazed
He felt ecstatic and amazed.
To a Pacific dawn he woke
Elated, eloquent, and broke.

And so his wandering life began:
He was a farm hand, dairyman,
An orange picker, lumberjack,
Dug tunnels for a trolley track,
Became a hobo and a bum,
Slept on the ground, his cold limbs numb;
At farm doors tried to cadge a meal,
And even chewed banana peel.

In bunks he felt the bed bugs bite,
And in his notebooks tried to write.
His mates found this a bit dismaying,
But they enjoyed his banjo playing.

He finally rejoined the ranks
Of humble clerks who toil in banks;
And soon they said, to Robert's joy:
"You're going to the Yukon, boy!"

By boat to Skagway, then by rail,
He followed that old Gold Rush Trail.
In Whitehorse for three years he stayed —
The brightest move he ever made.

For there, the gateway to the North,
Sourdoughs to him their tales poured forth
Of Gold Rush Times, of bar-room fights,
Of gaudy, bawdy days and nights,
Of booze and broads, ferocious feuds,
Grafters and gamblers and dudes,
Of gold dust gleaming in the pan
And Mounties, out to get their man,
Of strange things done in the midnight sun
—And Robert noted every one.

He noted too, with style and grace,
The wild, white beauty of the place.
He'd walk on snowshoes through the night,
The far, cold moon his only light;
And as he walked with quiet tread
The verses came into his head.

Soon Dan McGrew had been created
And frozen Sam McGee cremated;
But in a cupboard, put away,
They didn't see the light of day.
At last he thought: "This makes no sense —
I'll publish, at my own expense."

The publisher sent back his money;
"Your verse," he said, "is fine and funny!"
So out that first slim volume came:
Songs of a Sourdough was its name.
It brought its author instant fame —
And fortune, for the writing game
Earned more than many a Gold Rush claim.

But Robert was a thrifty feller —
He kept his bank job as a teller.
To Dawson City he transferred;
The Klondike too his name had heard.
His new mates, bowing to his skill,
Cried: "Here's the Bard of Bawdyville!"

And in the mess, that bunch of boys
Would whoop it up with so much noise
That Robert then could only write
Well after midnight every night.

He left the bank and closed his till,
But, keen to stay in Dawson still,
He found a cabin on a hill.
There, walking he would often go
At seventy-two degrees below,
With icicles upon his breath

And danger of a frostbite death.

There, washing sometimes wasn't nice,
Rubbing down with chunks of ice.
Yet Robert Service thought it great,
And wrote The Trail of '98.

For many years he wrote his tales,
Long after he had left those trails.
And in those Klondike tales he told,
He truly struck a vein of gold.

Those characters delight us still:
There's Chewed-Ear Jenkins, Barb-Wire Bill,
And all that brash and boisterous crew:
The Ragtime Kid, and Dan McGrew,
And Sam McGee who warmed right through,
And, of course, the Lady known as Lou.

Though long before these fine creations,
The living culture of First Nations
Had viewed this land with subtle eyes
And shaped their arts to match its size,
Woven webs of songs and stories
Harmonized with all its glories.

Service was first to use with pride
The English language, versified,
To conjure up with joy and zest
The wild ways of his new-found West.

Since then, Canadians present
A literary firmament,

Where John McRae his talent wields
While poppies grow in Flanders Fields,
And Leacock, the economist,
Becomes a famous humorist.

Before him, Haliburton came:
His Clockmaker, Sam Slick by name,
Gained international acclaim.
While Pauline Johnson got together
Her poetry, in Flint and Feather,
And Lucy Maud Montgomery's Anne
Her sparkling careeer began.

Later, novelists arose
Whose names now everybody knows.
Robertson Davies earned high praise
With essays, stories, books and plays,
And the tales of Margaret Laurence
Brought her praise in mighty torrents.

Mordecai Richler, most provoking,
Makes people ask how much he's joking.
And lively too was the arrival
Of Margaret Atwood's book, Survival.
Her verse and novels are a hit
In all Canadian English Lit.
When she describes the bush, we find
She also maps the human mind.

Alice Munro touches our hearts
With all her storyteller's arts.
Michael Ondaatje never shirks
Delving where myth or marvel lurks,

And Farley Mowat's loved, it's clear,
Not just by People of the Deer.

For Carol Shields, no honour fits her
Better than prizes like Pulitzer:
That's where her fine Stone Diaries took her —
And it was listed for the Booker!

The reading public too are certain
To hail the works of Pierre Berton.
To The Last Spike he never fails
To keep the show upon the rails.

The list of works and those who write 'em
Goes on and on, ad infinitum,
Too rich and vast to classify
(Unless of course you're Northrop Frye) —
Which shows the future's safe and sure
For good Canadian literature,
So full of power and wit and radiance —
Here's to all literary Canadians!

COMPETITIVE ODIOUS ODES?

NELLIE McCLUNG
(1876 – 1951)

*(Nellie McClung grew up in Manitoba where she became a teacher, was active
in the women's suffrage movement and wrote a best-selling novel. With her
pharmacist husband and five children she went to live in Winnipeg, where her
forthright campaigning style made her a popular leader and the bane of the
Establishment. She was one of the five women in the 'Persons Case', challenging
the bizarre law which said that women were not legally 'persons')*

We owe much to Nellie McClung,
A campaigner creative and keen:
A battling feminist since she was young,
She transformed the political scene.

In Winnipeg, Nellie was leader
Of a specially formed delegation.
They went to the Premier, hoping he'd heed her
And give votes to the whole population.

The Premier was called Rodmond Roblin
(In fact, he'd the title of Sir.)
And he'd really much rather give votes to a goblin
Than Nellie and people like her.

As she spoke, his brain started to fizz
And he barked: "She is getting my goat.
A hyena in petticoats, that's what she is!
Nice women have no wish to vote."

Dismissed, Nellie said: "We can't wait,
So we'll stage a Mock Parliament then –

And the topical motion we'll choose to debate
Is "Should there be voting for men?"

Nellie spoke in the Premier's voice;
She said: "Men are as noble as kings –
It only unsettles them, having a choice –
Votes would make them uneasy, poor things!"

Her Parliament caused much hilarity
And some furious insults as well.
Her critics attacked her for sneering vulgarity,
Her supporters gave cheers for "Our Nell."

When the Liberals came on the scene
They decided to back Nellie's cause.
Manitoba was first, back in 1916,
To pass new equality laws.

The Assembly burst into song
When the suffrage decision was made.
The women's campaign had been bruising and long
And Nellie had led the crusade.

New battles remained to be fought:
The "Persons Case" soon would arrive.
By the *Famous Five* women the case had been brought,
And Nellie was one of the five.

That victory won, Nellie still didn't rest,
As well as being mother and wife,
For reforms and for justice with zeal and with zest
She campaigned for the rest of her life.

LAWREN HARRIS
(1885 – 1970)

*(Born in Brantford, Ontario, where his family's Massey-Harris Company
was based, Lawren Harris studied art in Toronto and Berlin before
becoming an artillery officer in World War One. He returned to Canada
and was one of the founders of the Group of Seven, the artists
who chose the wilderness landscapes of Canada as their subject,
and whose controversial exhibitions revolutionized Canadian art.)*

Before the Group of Seven came,
Canadian art was rather tame:
Portraits and pastures, grazing cows,
Little excitement could arouse.

Although the paintings were sedate
The frames were splendidly ornate.
Their owners' pleasure was intensive:
The pictures all looked so expensive.

Young painters came along, whose art
Would soon upset the applecart.
Tom Thomson was among the first –
Upon the art scene he would burst
With rugged landscapes setting forth
The wildest splendours of the North.

Lawren Harris was his friend –
Together they would go and spend
With other artists, many weeks
Camping among the lakes and peaks,
Sketching and painting what they saw –
A land magnificent and raw.

Now Harris was that creature rare:
An artist who had cash to spare.
He numbered in his family tree
The Massey-Harris Company.

A studio building was erected
Where struggling artists he selected
Could have a place to come and paint.
Tom Thomson said; "My style that ain't!
Really, for me it's much too grand."
Lawren said: "Tom, I understand.
We'll fit you out a little shack
Just like a cabin, at the back."

Though four years later, Thomson drowned,
His influence was still profound:
So seven painters of like mind
In one campaigning group combined.
To jolt the art world was their mission

With their first startling exhibition.
And so in those Toronto halls
Their paintings glowed upon the walls
With brush-strokes bold and colours blazing
In scenes where not one cow was grazing,
But clouds came tumbling down the skies
And stark and jagged trees did rise
Against the snow and ancient stone
Of lands uncharted and unknown.

Such pictures, rarely seen before,
Caused instantly a great furor,
And these artistic pioneers

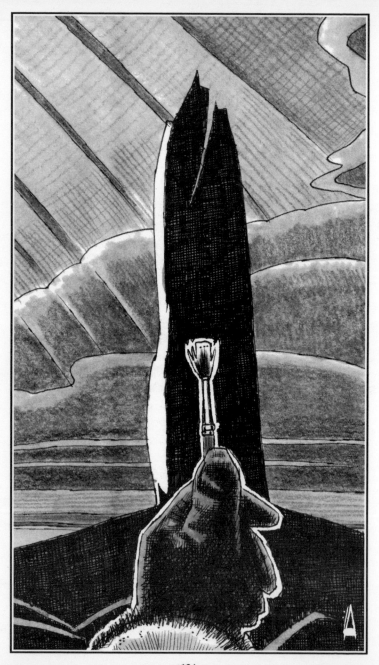

Were greeted with abuse and sneers.
For epithets the critics forage:

One said: "They're like hot mush or porridge!"
Another critic found a new lash:
"They should be called Hungarian Goulash!"

Not everyone was thinking so:
Debate was raging to and fro
And Lawren Harris said: "The fighting
Is all great fun, and quite exciting.
Canadian Art, in all this strife,
At least is showing signs of life!"

Soon other critics had their say
In England and the U.S.A.:
Triumphant praises came their way,
And now the Group had come to stay.

At home, the old tradition's faction
Went on to fight a rearguard action;
But more shows marked the Group's success
And left the critics in distress.
Soon they'd expand, and found with pride
A group of painters, nation-wide.

Now Lawren Harris would impart
More abstract features to his art:
Majestic icebergs, lakes of white,
And frozen peaks that tower in height.

He looked back on what he believed
The Group of Seven had achieved:

They set Canadian artists free
To paint the noble land they see.
Their art would be, for their own nation,
An endless act of re-creation.

DR. NORMAN BETHUNE
(1890 – 1939)

(Norman Bethune was born in Gravenhurst, Ontario, where his family home is now kept as a memorial museum. He was wounded in the First World War, then completed his medical studies and became a surgeon. He was unconventional and inventive, and believed passionately in medicine for all. His socialist outlook led him to go to the battlefront in the Spanish Civil War, and later to join Mao Tse-tung's army in China.)

Norman Bethune began his life
Son of a minister and his wife,
And their religion, they'd insist,
Was fervently evangelist.

Perhaps this background made him feel
An almost missionary zeal.
His mission was to cure and heal,
And he pursued this strong vocation
With life-long, fiery dedication.

After his war-time service, he
A surgeon would set out to be.
He married, travelled, settled down
At a big hospital in town:
There in Detroit, his fate looked grim –
Tuberculosis came to him.

During his treatment he suggested
That an experiment be tested:
There was a surgical technique
Which TB sufferers could seek.
The chest was opened, and in there

The surgeon started blowing air.

So Norman asked the powers-that-be:
"Why don't you try this out on me?"
Reluctantly, the staff agreed;
He was convinced they would succeed.
In two months he was re-assured –
He found himself completely cured.

In Montreal he worked for years
As one of surgery's pioneers.
He did research, and for a spell
Invented instruments as well.
His style was thought unorthodox
And gave his colleagues several shocks.

Now Dr. Archibald, his boss,
Became at times extremely cross.
"Norman," he said, "it seems your creed
Is doing surgery at speed.
You take risks, and I'd even claim
That breaking records is your aim!"

Norman Bethune did not admire
The usual medical attire.
He said: "My colleagues, I confess,
Resemble in their way of dress
A cross between, in their tradition,
A Maitre d' and a mortician."

But he was seriously concerned
In medicine, that the poor were spurned.
Campaigning fiercely, he advised

That medicine should be socialized.

Then he was asked to lead a corps
And join the Spanish Civil War.
In Spain, much thanks and great esteem
Greeted his blood transfusion team.
In the front line, in mire and mud,
He gave the wounded soldiers blood.

This hard and dangerous work had tired him,
But then another cause inspired him:
In 1937 began
China's invasion by Japan.
Though some might think his plan was barmy,
He joined with Mao Tse-tung's Red Army.

There with the front-line troops once more
He battled through the trials of war,
Trained doctors there, and nurses too,
And operated all night through.
A finger-cut became infected
And septicaemia was suspected.
Though every remedy was tried,
There in the midst of war, he died.
A Chinese hero he became:
A hospital now bears his name.
A new stamp and a monument
Are part too of his testament.

And Chairman Mao Tse-tung, no less,
Paid tribute to his selflessness.
For such great deeds his name will stand
At home, and in that far-off land.

SIR FREDERICK BANTING
(1891 – 1941)

*(Born in Alliston, Ontario, Frederick Banting served in the
Army Medical Corps during the first World War, and then tried
unsuccessfully to establish a practice in London, Ontario.
While there he had an idea of a way to treat the then killer disease of
diabetes. He went to Toronto and was taken on by Professor J.J.R. Macleod,
and with him and two other scientists, Charles Best and Dr. J.B. Collip,
developed the extract called insulin which continues to save the lives
of countless diabetes sufferers all over the world.)*

Now diabetics everywhere
Their praises should be granting
To one who eased their dread disease:
His name was Frederick Banting.

In London in Ontario
He glumly said: "The fact is,
No patients come – I must be dumb
To try and run a practice!"

But one night when he tossed and turned
In sleepless desperation,
Into his mind there came a blinding
Flash of inspiration.

He jotted down some scribbled lines –
It was no thorough treatise –
But he was sure he'd found a cure
To deal with diabetes.

He cried: "This is a great idea –
I'll act upon it pronto;
And so I'm off to see the Prof
Researching in Toronto."

He went to J.J.R. Macleod
And said his plan of action
Was now to take some dogs and make
A pancreas extraction.

Macleod approved the new research
And so it came to pass
That many a pup must render up
Its canine pancreas.

"The cure is ready," Banting said,
"Let's call it Insulin.
And now get set, it's time to let
The human trials begin."

The first to have the treatment
Was a boy of just fourteen.
It wasn't long till he grew strong
And great success was seen.

The whole world's press was quick to praise
The four-man team's success.
Soon Banting's name gained lots of fame –
The others, somewhat less.

A knighthood, then the Nobel Prize
Made Frederick Banting proud,

Though he was mad because he had
To share it with Macleod.

He did give half the cash to Best –
Macleod with Collip shared.
So all the four could feel the score
Had justly been declared.

Canadian research had now
A world-wide reputation,
And Banting's name at length became
A credit to his nation.

MARY PICKFORD
(1893 – 1979)

*Mary Pickford was a flourishing child actress on the Canadian stage
until she went first to Broadway and then into movies, becoming one
of the most idolized stars of the silent screen.*

Born in Toronto, Gladys Smith
Became a cinematic myth.
The glamorous Gladys rose to fame
With Mary Pickford as her name.

When she was three, her father died.
"How shall we live?" her mother sighed.
And then at five, on theatre stages,
Young Gladys started earning wages.

The child star flourished — at fourteen
She entered on the Broadway scene.
Though in some films she'd take a part,
She felt that it demeaned her art.

D. W. Griffith was the man
With whom her film career began.
He was a most perceptive fella:
He picked her out for Cinderella.

Such waif-like roles there were aplenty:
Poor Little Rich Girl, Sweet and Twenty,
Oh, Uncle! and The Little Teacher —
In countless films did Mary feature.

In all her winsome, child-like parts
She broke the audiences' hearts.
And very soon, with growing fame,
The national Sweeheart she became.

But though her roles were coy and cute,
Her business sense was most astute.
She and her mother, it would seem,
Made up a great financial team.
Their entry to negotiations
Gave movie moguls palpitations.

From forty dollars every week,
Much higher earnings she would seek.
In just two years they sure got bigger:
Ten thousand weekly was the figure!

She was among the first to see
A star could ask a massive fee
And make the Studios agree.

The moguls couldn't win the fight:
It took, to get her contract right,
According to Sam Goldwyn's stricture,
Much longer than to make the picture!

In 1919, stars she knew —
Fairbanks and Chaplin, Griffith too —
With Mary thought they'd have a go
At forming their own Studio.

United Artists had appeared:
The movie moguls scoffed and sneered.

"The lunatics" — as one did style 'em —
"Have taken over the asylum!"

Mary and Douglas Fairbanks wed,
And many gossip columns fed.
In lavish style they cut a dash
And made, and spent, a lot of cash.

A rambling mansion was the scene
Where they both reigned like King and Queen.
Pickford and Fairbanks thought they'd let it
Be called the name of PICKFAIR — get it?!

And still the audiences raved
For Mary in the roles they craved:
So impish, innocent, demure —
A Pollyanna, sweet and pure.
Mary was typecast, to her rage,
And frozen at that girlish age.

She said: "I'll show they've had their day,
These simpering maidens I portray —
I'll get my ringlets cut away!"
She did — and if you want to see 'em,
They're in a Hollywood museum.

Mary Pickford still survived
When talking pictures first arrived.
An early Oscar she would get
To praise her acting in Coquette.

Mary was nearly forty now,
And soon she made her final bow.
A Western was the last we'd see
Of her, in 1933.

At Grauman's Theater, where stars went
To put their prints in the cement,
Smaller than any, Mary's pair
Of tiny hands are frozen there:
Memorials to Gladys Smith,
Canadian cinematic myth.

BILLY BISHOP
(1894 – 1956)

*Born in Owen Sound, Ontario, Billy Bishop was an
unruly student who came into his own as an ace fighter pilot
during the First World War. He shot down a record 72 enemy planes and won
many medals, including the Victoria Cross. His courage and his flamboyant
personality made him a popular celebrity, and he lived to play an important role
with the Royal Canadian Air Force in World War Two.*

No great delight young Billy found
In life at school in Owen Sound;
Nor did he seem to get much knowledge
At Kingston's Military College.

By discipline he was repelled –
In fact, he nearly got expelled.
But Billy said: "Before you bar me,
I'm going off to join the army!"

He went to England then to train.
Drilling one day, in mud and rain,
He saw above, a fighter plane.
High up it flew, alone and free;
Billy decided: "That's for me!
This army life is such a chore:
I'll join the Royal Flying Corps."

Many Canadians shared his aim:
As pilots, twenty thousand came.

Now Billy, zooming through the air,
Was brave and brash and debonair.
Down through the clouds his plane would swoop
Then nonchalantly loop the loop.
He chased his quarries with ferocity
Pursuing them at high velocity;
He'd dart and dive, machine-guns blazing –
His accuracy was amazing.

His style was just a bit ham-handed –
He damaged aircraft when he landed.
One general was a bit dismayed
When Billy, undercarriage splayed,
Crashed right in front of his parade.

One colleague said: "Though Billy's got
Great talent as a brilliant shot
An expert pilot he is not!"

But though he was inclined to crash
He had such daring and panache
His score of planes shot down was higher
Than any other Air Force flyer.
He once shot five down in one day –
And many medals came his way.

And somehow Billy did contrive
Through years of war, to stay alive.
Home as a hero then he came
To celebrations, cheers and fame.

The war was won, but Billy still
Craved the excitement and the thrill.
A company he put in place
With Billy Barker, fellow ace.

They said: "What Torontonians need
To start their weekends off with speed
Are aircraft fitted with pontoons
To land on lakes among the loons.
We'll save them hours and hours of driving
And soon our service will be thriving!"

But then they squandered any gains
By buying two old fighter planes
To use their flying skills at once
At fairs and shows, by doing stunts.

Sadly, the first big show to hire them
Immediately had to fire them:
The pilots, feeling blithely manic,
Dived at the grandstand, causing panic.

Then, though the thrills and spills were less,
In business sales, he had success.
In World War Two, his reputation
Enthused the Air Force of the nation.

His fame and talent were well suited
To get Canadians recruited,
And Billy Bishop would be partial
To recognition as Air Marshal.
No fitter honour could be found
To praise the boy from Owen Sound.

JOHN DIEFENBAKER
(1895 – 1979)

*(John Diefenbaker spent his childhood in Ontario and in the
North West Territories, and came to Saskatchewan with his family at the age of
fifteen. He became a successful lawyer there, but always had political
ambitions. He eventually won a federal seat, and went on to lead the Progressive
Conservatives to power with the biggest majority in Canada's history.)*

John's mother asked him, as she eyed
Her little boy with loving pride:
"What do you think you'd like to be?"
"I'll be Prime Minister," said he.

Though he'd achieve his goal, he knew it,
It took him sixty years to do it.
He'd many failures when he ran
For office in Saskatchewan,
But finally he got selected
And was, surprisingly, elected.
For though the Tories had to meet
In 1940, mass defeat,
John Diefenbaker won a seat.

Later, his sixtieth birthday past,
He won the leadership at last
And dealt the Liberals a blow
In two elections in a row.

Fiercely he tore his foes asunder:
His oratory rolled out like thunder
And with his great charisma, Dief
Deserved his title as The Chief.

And yet some critics would insist:
"He's just a Prairie Populist –
His words are humbug and flapdoodle,
The pompous prattle of a noodle!"

Dief promised Canada would see
A rendezvous with destiny.
A noble vision he set forth,
A great new Canada of the North!
Some wondered, though it sounded grand,
Where else he could locate the land?

Justice it's true made many a gain
During John Diefenbaker's reign.
He stopped the harsh discrimination
In quotas set for immigration.

Votes came for each First Nation race
And their first Senator took his place.
Dief was the first P.M. to set
A woman in the Cabinet,
And boldly too he set his sights
On a Canadian Bill of Rights.

And yet, in many people's eyes,
The Chief in power was a surprise.
Though Liberals' control had withered,
John Diefenbaker flapped and dithered.

The Arrow jet which could provide
A symbol of Canadian pride
Was scrapped by Dief because of cost
And fourteen thousand jobs were lost.

The planes were junked, though rumours say
One was kept hidden to this day,
And flies in secret once a year.
Not very credible, we fear:
The rumours also claim it's clear,
In tales as fanciful as Chaucer's,
The factory also made flying saucers!

Dief clashed with Kennedy, made it known
He wanted a non-nuclear zone,
Bought U.S. planes which stayed unused
When nuclear warheads he refused.
By Cuba too he was confused,
And Kennedy was most derisive
When Dief's response was indecisive.

Financially he could be blind:
The Governor of the Bank resigned,
And Dief would make the nation holler
When he devalued Canada's dollar.

Then Parliament, the outlook grim,
Voted No Confidence in him.
John had achieved his boyhood mission
But now he leads the Opposition.
His lurid language he parades
In fierce and furious tirades.

Into his eighties he would be
A fervent federal M.P.,
Attracting with advancing age
Warmth and respect instead of rage:
John Diefenbaker now with pleasure
Had turned into a national treasure!

NORMA SHEARER
(1900 – 1983)

(Norma Shearer grew up in Montreal, and from there her mother brought her to New York and then to Hollywood, to get her into films. She became a star, and married the movie mogul Irving Thalberg, one of the bosses of M.G.M.)

At the age of just fourteen
Young Norma was a beauty queen
And then a popular child model;
Her mother said: "This is a doddle!
Destined for fame you surely are –
You're going to be a movie star!"

So in New York they went to town –
The Ziegfeld Follies turned her down
And so an extra she became
And had some bit parts to her name.

Then a tycoon in Hollywood
Said; "This girl could be really good."
Now Irving Thalberg was the man
Who first became a Shearer fan.
He'd soon become a powerful player -
A boss of Metro-Goldwyn-Mayer.

To California she'd go
To screen-test at the studio.
On first seeing Thalberg, quite unwary,
She thought he was a secretary –
For even in those early days
Norma had hoity-toity ways.

Her screen-test chance she nearly lost:
One of her eyes was slightly crossed
And a producer also chose
To comment on her bumpy nose.

So Louis Mayer then said No.
Her face all wet with tears of woe
She pleaded for another go.

Mayer relented – one small part
At least would give the girl a start;
And in the rushes he detected
A quality he'd not expected:
She looked intense, still and demure,
And unlike some stars, even pure!

Now launched upon the movie scene
In those days of the silent screen,
Her repertoire of parts grew wider:
She even played a bareback rider.
Thalberg was always there beside her
To choose her roles and groom and guide her.

Soon, there were roses and romance,
And many a night they'd dine and dance.
The *Yes Sir! That's My Baby* tune
Was making Norma Shearer swoon,
But they were rarely quite alone:
Her mother came, as chaperone.
That is perhaps why Irving chose
To speed the courtship, and propose.

Their wedding, lavish, loud and glittering,
Had all the gossip columns twittering.
The gossips said, with deadly charm:
"This will do her career no harm!"

Norma indeed achieved her goal
And played in many a starring role.
She was endearingly petite
At just one inch above five feet.
She made the audiences love her
While leading men all towered above her.

Laughton and Tyrone Power were two;
The first moustache Clark Gable grew
Was for a film with Norma Shearer
And brought his super-stardom nearer.

She won an Oscar, and would get
Star roles in *Marie Antoinette*
And *Romeo and Juliet*.

But while the fans she was bewitching
The other female stars were bitching.
She made Joan Crawford very cross –
Joan said: "You're never at a loss
When you are sleeping with the boss!"

Her enmity was unremitting:
For Norma's close-ups, Joan was sitting
Blithely beside the camera, knitting.

Her rivals Norma would condemn:
She was the Queen of M.G.M.

And Norma Shearer wasn't kidding
When telling staff to do her bidding.

She sent for stylish clothes one day
And ordered Wardrobe staff to stay
And spend all night, with much impatience,
To make a set of imitations.
She sent the originals, what's more,
Right back, unpaid for, to the store.

At 37, Thalberg died,
And vainly Norma Shearer tried
To keep her queenly status still.
There were disputes about the will,
And Louis Mayer soon would show
That he could be a ruthless foe.

Then Norma wed her ski instructor
Who from her widow's status plucked her,
And Norma left the movie scene.
But still remembered she has been.
Websites and memorabilia are
Constant reminders of the star
Who left Quebec to find she could
Become a Queen in Hollywood.

WINNIE THE POOH

The origins of A.A.Milne's famous character can be traced back to a Canadian bear cub which became a First World War army mascot.

The Second Infantry Brigade
By train a wartime journey made:
White River in Ontario
Was on the route they had to go,
And Captain Colebourn spotted there
A most enchanting baby bear.

The Captain promptly thought he'd get
The little black cub as a pet.
He said, "I'll mark my home town's fame
By making Winnipeg its name."

Soon known as Winnie, she was made
The mascot of the whole brigade.
In England where they went to train
They had a camp on Salisbury Plain.
Winnie was petted, praised and fed,
And slept beneath the Captain's bed.

But when the troops went off to war
Winnie could stay with him no more.
The Zoo was asked, for the duration,
To give the bear accommodation.

Soon, capering around her cage
Winnie the bear was all the rage.
She'd roll around and wave her paws
And revel in the crowd's applause.

The Captain, when the war had ended,
Thought Winnie's winning ways were splendid.
It would be best for her, he knew,
To leave her there in London Zoo.

The children loved her - there was one
Called Christopher, A.A.Milne's young son,
Who at the age of five or six
Was just delighted with her tricks.

His father wrote, to please the boy,
A tale that children would enjoy
In which a teddy bear did feature;
Winnie was what he called the creature,
After the bear in London Zoo
And so was born Winnie the Pooh.

The real bear died in quiet old age -
Her namesake though still holds the stage,
Alive and kicking on the page.

White River in commemoration
Now holds an annual celebration
To honour Captain Colebourn's name
And that young cub who rose to fame:
Winnie, the bear who gained such glory
By starring in a children's story.

FAY WRAY
(Born 1907)

*(Alberta-born Fay Wray moved as a child with her family
to California where she soon got parts in movies as an extra and then
in more major roles. She was able to make the transition from silent films
to talkies, and had her big screen success in the celebrated monster movie,
King Kong – a role which has tended to overshadow the many
other achievements of her long lifetime)*

Fay Wray was born, as one of six,
In what some cynics call The Sticks.
Near Cardston in Alberta, Fay
First came to see the light of day.

The family moved south, and Fay
Was happy living in L.A.
For that was where the films were made,
The centre of the movie trade.

Just in her teens, Fay Wray was seen
In Westerns on the silent screen:
A winsome heroine, with lots
Of noiseless hooves and silent shots –
Rescued of course, for plots don't vary,
By gallant cowboys on the prairie.

And soon the talent scouts would cast her
With Janet Gaynor, Mary Astor
And other starlets, to be some
Of movies' greats in years to come.

Von Stroheim's *Wedding March* became
The film that launched her into fame.

What's more, it got her off the ground
With a career in films with Sound.

When Talking Pictures first arrived
Not every silent screen star thrived,
For some of them were heard to speak
With voices like a croak or squeak.

But Fay Wray's talking passed the test,
And then she found she was the best
At one sound more than all the rest:
Fay Wray became the *Queen of Scream*,
 The Horror-Movie-Maker's dream!

The movie-goers flocked to see 'em:
The Vampire Bat, *The Wax Museum*,
And many more – the fans, she knew,
Were terrified, and deafened too.

And then her big chance came along
To co-star with the ape, *King Kong*.
That hairy and primeval monster
In filmdom's Hall of Fame ensconced her.

The great adventure story features
An island full of giant creatures
Who lived a million years before us:
Triceratops and Stegosaurus –
All fierce and furious and strong,
But none of them a match for Kong.

The island tribe who kidnap Fay
Give her to Kong as luscious prey.

As fearful in his cave she nestles
The giant ape goes out and wrestles:
No jungle creature there can match him
But humans find a way to catch him.

He's gassed and captured, brought away
And in New York put on display.
But Kong, escaping from his cage,
Goes on a city-wide rampage;
And where is Fay? She's far from calm
Clutched in his tender, hairy palm.

And really, no-one could expect her
To know he's trying to protect her!
Where can Kong go, to flee his fate?
Where else, but up the Empire State?
While Fay is screaming, loud and long,
The planes attack, and conquer Kong.

The movie, when it went on show,
Made millions for the studio.
So hectic then was Fay's career
She made – astonishing to hear –
Eleven movies in one year.

She was a film director's wife
And led a star's luxurious life:
A mansion, cocktails, tea and tennis –
And largely thanks to King Kong's menace.

She went on making films, retired,
Came back, remaining much admired,
Wrote books, and dramas for the stage,

And then at ninety years of age
This star who had her name in lights
Was lobbying for writers' rights.

Alberta's girl had made the grade
In glitzy Hollywood's parade,
And movie fans still love to gape
At Fay and her gigantic ape.

JOSEPH-ARMAND BOMBARDIER
(1908-1964)

From his teenage years Bombardier showed his creative skill with machinery,
and went on to invent the snowmobile and the ski-doo, and to found
the internationally successful company that still bears his name.

All through his childhood and his teens
Bombardier just loved machines.
While other less ingenious boys
Were playing ball or breaking toys
Young Armand's interest was greater
In fiddling with the carburator.
He thought kids' games were just for mugs -
He'd rather clean the sparking plugs.

His father, thinking him a star,
Said, "What a clever lad you are!
So here's an ancient car, my son -
Dismantling it could be fun."

So Armand, grateful to his dad,
Embarked on an idea he had.
He planned a vehicle to go
With passengers, across the snow.

He took the engine out, and fit
Four ski-like runners under it.
Then, being a most inventive feller,
He built himself a large propeller.
With this he would, such was his plan,
Replace the radiator fan.

"Allons, mon petit frère!" he told
His younger brother, Léopold.
Said Armand, "I'll be on the back
To keep the vehicle on track
While at the front end, brother dear,
You sit and use your feet to steer."

Then after each took up his perch
The strange device began to lurch
And judder forward, slowly sliding,
The brothers perilously riding.

Along the snowbound streets they went
Creating great astonishment.
The folk of Valcourt in Quebec
Thought one at least would break his neck.

They zigged and zagged from side to side
While gleefully young Armand cried:
"I had a dream and made it real,
And here it is - the Snowmobile!"

Knowing his genius was large
His father built him a garage
And here with purpose unrelenting
Bombardier went on inventing -
Learned English too, so he could read
The science journals he would need.

The Snowmobile he engineered
Had tracks, and skis in front that steered.
He toured Quebec to flaunt its glories
And featured much in front-page stories.

It met with widespread admiration,
Transforming winter transportation.
Doctors and priests and rescue crews,
The postal service bearing news
And many more, found great appeal
In Armand's wondrous Snowmobile.

Then he devised a new machine:
The Ski-Doo zoomed upon the scene.
A zippy, zappy new sensation,
A must for winter recreation.

His company went on to do
Trains, aeronautics, sea-doos too -
And, honouring Bombardier's fame
The company still bears his name.

Yet no advance in transportation
Could match the wild exhilaration
Of that first journey through the snow
One day in Valcourt, long ago.

PIERRE TRUDEAU
(1919-2000)

*Flamboyant Montreal lawyer Pierre Trudeau became Prime Minister
in 1968 and led the country for most of the following sixteen years,
during which he was both idolized and reviled, but never ignored.*

Cultured and cool and charismatic,
Pierre's career was never static.
One of the Liberals' leading lights,
He led them up towards the heights;
Then as he basked upon the summit,
His popularity would plummet.
And when it looked like he'd been trounced,
Back to the top he promptly bounced.

Pierre grew up in Montreal;
A schoolboy essay he'd recall:
"What do you want to be?" He thought:
Seaman...? Explorer...? Astronaut...?
(They'd laugh if he had written: "I've
A plan to move to Sussex Drive.")

But Law was what he wound up doing,
And on vacations, went canoeing.
The doctorate plans which he unfurled
Meant travelling around the world —
And so with backpack and with beard
The Hippie Trail he pioneered,
And foiled a knife attacker's bid
While climbing up a Pyramid.
(A useful skill in later life
In worlds where back-stabbing is rife.)

Back home, he saw the great appeal
Of Révolution Tranquille.
The Liberal Party wooed him then
As one of Québec's Three Wise Men.
So, somewhat to his own surprise,
Began his meteoric rise.

Just two years after his election
He stood for leadership selection.
The Old Guard said: "He'll cause us scandals —
The guy wears coloured shirts, and sandals!
Voters will never choose Pierre —
They'd rather have a grizzly bear!"

But they were wrong, that diehard band,
For Trudeaumania swept the land.
It gave the party such a boost,
Soon Pierre Trudeau ruled the roost.
It was the Liberals' finest hour:
The red rose had begun to flower.

The Right looked on with some anxiety
As Trudeau launched his Just Society.
He then said: "Though you may berate us,
We're giving French official status.
The Anglophones must mend their ways
And recognize La Langue Française."

It's no surprise the Opposition
Did not share Trudeau's sense of mission.
He called them "nobodies", a phrase
They hardly took as lavish praise.

One day he mouthed a certain word
In mime, so it could not be heard.
When asked, so there should be no muddle,
What was it? He said: "Fuddle Duddle!
Or really racily, it may be
I might have told you, Fuddle Dee Dee!"

For sixteen years Pierre would reign,
Although his star would wax and wane.
Once, when faintly it did burn,
For nine months, Joe Clark took a turn.

Pierre was showy and dramatic,
Though critics called him autocratic.
"His style," said one, "though he's a stayer,
Makes Judas seem a good team player."

But now and then he got it wrong
With slogans like THE LAND IS STRONG,
To which the voters, like as not,
Were apt to yawn and say: "So what?"

Advisers, in his third campaign,
Said: "Margaret, please don't join the train."
That view she said she would defy;
She called Pierre a loving guy,
And crowds all cheered her to the sky.
But politics would take their toll —
She'd go elsewhere to rock and roll.

Pierre's career went rolling on;
Sometimes he struggled, sometimes shone.
Once, in a ploy both cute and neat,

He engineered his own defeat,
Another time resigned, and then
Decided to come back again.

His progress sometimes could be chequered,
And very nearly got Quebecer'd.
He found it hard to keep in check
The separatists in Quebec,
Tried to maintain a plural nation
And keep them in the Federation —
While other provinces, no doubt,
Were quite inclined to boot them out.

But he survived, to sweat and toil
To solve the crisis over oil,
And eat his words, and eat them whole,
On needs for wage and price control.

But Trudeau, still the clever mover,
The Gang of Eight would outmanoeuvre
And greet with triumph and elation
The Constitution's patriation.

He thought he'd closed that "can of worms",
And later spoke in scathing terms
Of those who opened it to make
Supposed improvements at Meech Lake
And an Accord at Charlottetown.
But then the voters turned them down.

Whether Pierre was loved, or hated,
His style was never understated.

And round the world as he gyrated,
He made quite sure, when he was fêted,
That Canada was highly rated.

Pierre's one of the brighter gems
In lists of Canada's P.M.'s.
Sir John MacDonald was the first —
A great man, with a greater thirst.
He found at last he couldn't handle
The great Pacific Railway scandal.

Then came Mackenzie (Alexander)
A man who was immune to slander.

Translating Gettysburg's Address
Was Wilfrid Laurier, no less —
Abe Lincoln he admired, we knew,
And much admired the ladies too.

The twentieth century would bring
William Lyon Mackenzie King:
The longest serving leader, he
Had one great eccentricity,
For by Ouija board he tried
To reach folks on the Other Side;
His mother, so he claimed, replied.

And then there was rumbustious Dief,
Conservatives' impressive Chief.
Stanfield and Meighen and Joe Clark
To lead the country would embark.
Each made a great or lesser mark.

Lester Pearson did so well,
He got the Peace Prize from Nobel.
From him the leadership would go
Eventually to Pierre Trudeau.

Then Brian Mulroney wheeled and dealed
And quite a fashion sense revealed.
And for a short while, after him,
We caught the briefest glimpse of Kim.

Jean Chrétien took up the fight —
He was a Trudeau acolyte,
So once again the torch could flare
In tribute to the great Pierre!

RENÉ LÉVESQUE
(1922 – 1987)

René Lévesque was a celebrated broadcaster before he entered politics
as a Liberal. He later founded the Parti Québécois which was victorious
in two elections but just failed in 1980 to get a referendum majority
in favour of an independent Quebec.

Though he was small, René Lévesque
Was walking tall throughout Quebec,
Becoming, after many a schism,
The Champion of Separatism.

When he was young, he'd no ambition
To be a party politician.
A war reporter he became –
Then Radio-Canada made his name:
His style and passion brought him fame.

That fame would help him, it was clear,
In a political career;
And so he won a Liberal seat
And joined the Cabinet elite.

At first he backed with resolution
Lesage's Quiet Revolution.
But soon Lévesque would change his tone
And start to strike out on his own,
Fiercely proclaiming to the crowd
A revolution much more loud.

The Parti Québécois was founded
And drums for independence sounded.
Supporters proudly would recall
The words of General de Gaulle:
"Vive le Québec Libre!" was his call
Delivered from the City Hall
When he arrived in Montreal.

It took some years before Lévesque
Was able to persuade Quebec
To opt, in 1976,
For René's brand of politics.

And oh, what rage and consternation
Was felt that day across the nation –
Or anyway, in Ottawa
Where René caused a brouhaha!
He told them, when he heard them yelp:
"A tranquilliser ought to help!"

(Yet there were always those out west
Who thought Quebec was such a pest
It wouldn't really drive them frantic
To see it sink in the Atlantic ...)

But René didn't do his worst:
He played it very cool at first,
And talked not of a separate nation,
But "Sovereignty-Association."
This helped his devious intent,
Since no one knew quite what it meant.

René announced, being worldly-wise,
That he'd maintain the federal ties
And promised that he wouldn't end 'em
Until he'd held a Referendum.

He managed to procrastinate
About the question, and the date;
When they were fixed, Quebec would see
Intense campaigns for Non and Oui.

Across the province, to and fro,
They watched the heavy hitters go,
Jean Chrétien and Pierre Trudeau,
Urging the case for voting No.

Although Quebeckers as a whole
Resented federal control,
Sixty per cent of voters stated
They'd no wish to be separated.

Yet when the P.Q. won again
Lévesque's power soon began to wane,
And resignations would conspire
To make him ready to retire.

And now, although Lévesque is gone,
The fights he fought still rumble on.

OSCAR PETERSON
(Born 1925)

*Born in Montreal, Oscar Peterson was already playing in bands
and on the radio when he was in his teens. With his flamboyant style
and personality, he soon went on to achieve world-wide popularity and to
play with, and be admired by, all the greatest jazz musicians.*

Oscar, as a virtuoso,
Made other pianists seem just so-so.
This boy who came to wow them all
From London to Carnegie Hall
Was born and raised in Montreal.

Oscar, like all the children, had
Good music lessons from his dad:
He was a porter by profession,
But music was his great obsession.
At school, young Oscar would astound
His fellow-students, gathered round
To hear his boogie-woogie sound.

He won at fourteen, easily,
A contest at the CBC
And soon in his own weekly show
Played piano on the radio.

He wanted to leave school to play;
His father let him have his way,
But said: "Son - be, unlike the rest,
Not just a player, but the Best!"

His father's words young Oscar heeded
And aiming for the top, succeeded.
He played with bands, made records too,
And soon his reputation grew.

Now Oscar got his greatest chance
When he was heard by Norman Granz.
The famous impresario
Declared: "I want you in my show.

Jazz at the Philharmonic's fame
Will very quickly make your name."
So at Carnegie Hall he played,
And what an impact there he made!
With Ray Brown on the double bass
He quite electrified the place.

From then on, his career was made -
In world-wide concert tours he played.
With Granz's troupe he would appear
In eighty cities in a year.

Crowds reveled at the expertise
Of this magician of the keys.
He seemed to play, his listeners reckoned,
At least a hundred notes a second.
One colleague said: "His pianos seem
So hot, they give off smoke and steam."

This suave and smiling, bear-like man
Was raved about by every fan.
The bracelet that he'd always wear -

THE KING

A gift to him from Fred Astaire -
Dazzled, just like the watch he wore;
His music dazzled even more.

Practical jokes he played a lot
On colleagues, but revenge they got:
Stuck keys together, even hid
Steel balls inside the piano lid.

Arthritis plagued him, and he'd face
A lot of slurs upon his race.
In Canada he thought it bad
No black was in a TV ad;
Though that today seems very strange,
Oscar's campaign began the change.

At times some music critics panned him -
He said they couldn't understand him.
But though the critics might attack him,
His colleagues never failed to back him.

And Oscar played with all the greats
In Canada and in the States:
With Ella, Armstrong and Count Basie
And Dizzy, always acting crazy.
His various Trios reached the heights
Of challenge and of jazz delights.
Even Art Tatum was impressed
And Art, for Oscar, was the best.

As Oscar now recalls his story,
He ought to bask in all this glory.

A deluge of awards and praise
Honours the way that Oscar plays.

For as one music guru said
When asked: "Who would you like, when dead,
To be reincarnated as?" -
"I would be Oscar, King of Jazz!"

MARGARET LAURENCE
(1926 – 1987)

(Margaret Laurence was born in Neepawa, Manitoba.
Her mother and father both died before she was ten, and she was brought up
by her aunt and grandfather. From her childhood years she always wanted
to be a writer, and after going to university in Winnipeg, she married
Jack Laurence, a civil engineer, and lived abroad and in Vancouver
and Ontario, becoming Canada's most successful novelist.)

In Neepawa, Manitoba,
Margaret Laurence as a child
With the loss of both her parents
Never could be reconciled.

Through her life, although she hid it,
She was often insecure.
Writing gave her strength and purpose –
Of her talent she was sure.

Like her character Vanessa,
Maybe Margaret's childhood style
Featured pioneering epics
And romance beside the Nile.

When she went to university
It could surely be no crime
Reading novels in the bookstore
Just one chapter at a time.

Margaret was then beginning
On her own career in fiction.

"Writing" she declared with gusto,
"Is my permanent addiction!"

With Jack, the engineer she married,
She went travelling abroad.
In the Gold Coast and Somalia
Her imagination soared.

Africa, with all its richness,
As a setting served her well
In her books like *This Side Jordan*
And *The Prophet's Camel Bell*.

But her homeland was the setting
For the books that brought her fame,
And the town of Manawaka
Has become a household name.

There the battling Hagar Shipley,
Over ninety years of age,
Triumphing in male society,
Springs to life on every page.

There too, Rachel was a teacher:
A Jest of God a film became,
And her stories of Vanessa
Add to Manawaka's fame.

Margaret Laurence was outspoken
On the issues of the day,
And on race, or nuclear weapons,
She would loudly have her say.

From
Mogadishu
to
Manitoba...

LAURENCE of
MANAWAKA

Issues too of sexuality
Books like *The Diviners* spanned.
There were some who, in Ontario,
Would have liked to see it banned.

Others, though, were more perceptive:
With them, *The Diviners* scored.
The Governor General also praised it
And he gave her his Award.

Colleges and universities
Gave her many an accolade,
And the nation saw her portrait
On a postage stamp displayed.

GORDIE HOWE
(born 1928)

*Gordie Howe grew up in Saskatchewan, a hockey fanatic even as a child.
His genius was soon spotted by the Detroit Red Wings, for whom he played for
25 years. His career continued even after that, and his name appeared constantly
in the record books and is enshrined in Hockey's Hall of Fame.*

The countless fans of Gordie Howe
All thought their hero was a wow.
His hockey prowess showed up soon
Where he grew up in Saskatoon.

There Gordie learned to skate, we're told,
When he was only four years old.
At home, he practised day and night
Shooting with left hand and with right,
And sometimes made his parents grouse
By knocking shingles off the house.

Then by a scout the boy was seen
When he was only just sixteen.
Off to the Red Wings' Camp he'd go
At Windsor in Ontario.

At eighteen, making his debut
His first game saw his first goal too;
The first of many – he would score
In his career, a thousand more.

Bull-necked and burly, Gordie struck
With his fierce stick, not just the puck.

The other players sometimes found
That he had felled them to the ground.

With deadly skill he swooped and scythed
While on the ice his rivals writhed,
And those trapped in the corner knew
The power of Gordie's elbows too.

His whole career was nearly through
When he was only twenty-two:
He skidded, slipped and cracked his head –
Brain damage almost left him dead.
The surgeons saved him – just one trace
Remained – a tic that jerked his face.
His callous team-mates seemed to think he
Would revel in the nickname Blinky!

Soon Gordie's wounds had healed so well
He galvanized the NHL.
Eighty-six points would clearly sock it
To Gordie's runner-up, The Rocket.
His progress after that was stunning
As Scoring Champion four times running.

With Stanley Cups and MVP's
Gordie would lead the field with ease.
This hero, speedy and adroit,
Spent twenty-five years with Detroit.
But his career was not complete:
He managed an amazing feat.

At forty-five, he ruled the roost on
World Hockey's Aero team in Houston,
And – what would really gild the dream –
Gordie's two sons were on the team!

New England and Hartford Whalers too
Brought hockey challenges anew.

No wonder Gordie Howe's great name
Stands out in Hockey's Hall of Fame,
For in that Hall he earned his residence
Through terms of seven U.S. Presidents!

MAURICE "THE ROCKET" RICHARD
(1929-2000)

*One of fhe great hockey stars of all time, Maurice Richard played for the
Montreal Canadiens for nearly twenty years, broke many records and helped
the team to win eight Stanley Cups. He was so popular with the fans
that his suspension once caused a riot in the city.*

A Governor-General, called Lord Stanley,
Liked games that were robust and manly.
The fastest, toughest game, he thought,
Was Canada's great winter sport.

Ice hockey first began to thrive
Way back in 1855,
When someone grabbed a hockey stick
And cried: "Now, get your skates on, quick!
Though hockey on the grass is nice,
We'll play it faster on the ice."

It caught on quickly, and became
A favourite Canadian game.
Lord Stanley never ever tired
Of seeing the game he so admired.
He said: "I'd love to take it up,
But I'm an old dog, not a pup:
Instead, I shall present a Cup."

And so the Stanley Cup was made,
And for it fierce, fast games are played:
Tumultuous, titanic clashes

Where every player swerves and dashes
And swoops and darts and sometimes crashes.
Defeat and danger they defy,
Hoping to hold that trophy high.

Now, Hockey's crowded Hall of Fame
Resounds with many a famous name.
Among the greatest, many claim,
To reach the summit of the game
Rocket Richard's best of all —
Canadiens' star, in Montreal.

It was in 1942
The Rocket first soared into view,
And fans of the Canadiens
Watching him play, exclaimed: "Tiens!
Maurice va jouer très bien!"

And they were right — for eighteen years
The Forum rang with rapturous cheers
As, blazing forth in every game,
The Rocket really earned his name.

Just two years after he'd begun
The team sure made those Red Wings run:
The record score was 9 to 1.
A game to come was better still —
A play-off, won Eleven-Nil.

The Final of the Stanley Cup
In '52 lined two teams up:
Boston and Montreal were playing;
Canadiens' fans were surely praying —

They couldn't bear it if they lost on
Such a night, to rivals Boston.

Each team was full of brave defiance —
This was a battle of the giants.
The scores were even for a spell;
A heavy tackle — Maurice fell!
Knocked out and bloody, he revived —
The tie-break finally arrived.

The winning goal the Rocket scored:
Fans cheered the hero they adored.
The crowd stood up, and that ovation
Was four whole minutes in duration.

Many times since, those rival Bruins
Were left with their defence in ruins;
And there were lots of other teams
Who left the ice with shattered dreams.
Canadiens' goals inspired the Forum,
And Maurice knew just how to score 'em.

Richard his name has also lent
To one unfortunate event,
The Richard Riot, which we know
Was more than forty years ago.

A fight had happened on the ice —
Richard's behaviour wasn't nice.
Said Hockey's President: "Richard —
From all this season's games, you're barred!"

The President's decision came
The night before a Red Wings game.
The fans thought this appalling manners,
And marched the streets with protest banners.
President Campbell rashly came
To take his seat to watch the game.

The fans, who thought he was the dregs,
Threw ripe tomatoes, rocks and eggs.
By someone's fist he soon got hit,
And then a tear gas bomb was lit.
The place filled up with yellow smoke;
The crowd began to scream and choke.

The game was lost, the fans went out
And roared and raged and rushed about.
Windows were smashed, cars overturned,
Shops looted, and some buildings burned.
The rioting went on all night,
And left the city quite a sight.

Though Maurice wanted no such show
And asked for calm, on radio,
The Richard Riot always came
To be remembered with his name.

The next year, that same President
The Stanley Cup would soon present
To Maurice, for his winning team:
A nightmare turned into a dream.
And then, from there the team would go
To win four more Cups in a row.

More records saw him top the polls:
The first to get five hundred goals,
And first to score, of all great names,
His fifty goals in fifty games.
Eight Stanley Cups he helped to win;
First TV coverage he was in.

His reputation — none would knock it,
For there's been no one like The Rocket!

TIM HORTON
(1930 – 1974)

*(The founder of the famous chain of Tim Hortons coffee shops was born in
Cochrane, Ontario, and grew up to be a hockey star with a place in the
Hall of Fame. He played 24 seasons in the NHL, mainly with the
Toronto Maple Leafs. The first Tim Hortons store opened in Hamilton, Ontario,
in 1964, and the chain was already well established by the time
of his death in a car crash ten years later.)*

The Stanley Cup four times
Tim's team would claim,
And now a coffee cup maintains his fame.
The man whose name
Has helped the chain to thrive
Began playing hockey at the age of five.

At nineteen, pro games put him to the test:
The Pittsburgh Hornets took him to their nest;
And soon the Maple Leafs recruited Tim –
For eighteen years his star would never dim.

As a defenceman he was like a wall:
With body checks, opponents he would stall;
And Gordie Howe, a big Tim Horton fan,
Declared that he was Hockey's Strongest Man.

Now Tim, who had a family to support,
Wanted more income than he got from sport.
He said: "Hamburger restaurants, I guess,
Could be a recipe for great success."

They weren't, but Tim just wasn't going to stop:
Instead, he started up a doughnut shop.
In Hamilton, in 1964,
The first Tim Hortons opened up its door.

He put an ad into the press, to test
If someone else was ready to invest.
A Hamilton police constable, Ron Joyce,
Thought this would be a wise commercial choice.

So that was how the Hortons chain began:
Soon the Canadian nation it would span.
The route to being an icon Tim had taken,
Like maple syrup or Canadian bacon.
In those first days when ready cash was shorter,
A coffee and a doughnut cost a quarter.

The chain expanded,
And with business brilliance
It soon would count its revenue in millions.
Each eager patron, sipping coffee, savours
Doughnuts which have a dazzling range of flavours.

Tim with a light touch – though a heavy hitter –
Devised the Dutchie and the Apple Fritter.
In hockey too he showed imagination:
Some say the slap shot was his own creation.

Tim lived to see his chain of stores expand,
Spreading their cheery image through the land.
"Always Fresh" became their chosen motto.
One fervent fan compared them to a grotto,

A holy place where worshippers could boast
That they consumed a Timbit like the Host.

The chain's success, like everything commercial,
Attracted comments that were controversial.
Some said the freshness claim was over-stated,
And frozen doughnuts were resuscitated.
The firm was somewhat cagey in reply,
And said that "Always Fresh" did still apply.

There was another rumour to deny:
That in Tim Hortons' thriving doughnut trade,
The Timbit came from where the hole was made!

Today, although the firm has merged with Wendy's,
It still attracts traditionalists and trendies,
To whom Tim Hortons keeps with resolution
Its role as a Canadian institution,
And honours proudly this great player's name,
Just like his place in Hockey's Hall of Fame.

WILLIAM SHATNER
(born 1931)

(Born in Montreal, William Shatner started his acting career in the theatre and in films. Then he landed the television role of Captain Kirk in the Star Trek series, which made him an international – indeed an inter-galactic – star.)

Captain James Tiberius Kirk
Gave William Shatner years of work.
An actor really could do worse
Than flit around the universe
To distant worlds and alien skies
Upon the starship *Enterprise*,
Exchanging quips with Mr Spock
And planning where the ship will dock.

It all began in Montreal
Where William heard the theatre's call.
He played Tom Sawyer, we are told,
When he was only twelve years old,
Read Economics at McGill
And in revues revealed his skill.

Stratford, then Broadway, came along –
There was *The World of Suzie Wong*
And even Marlowe's *Tamburlaine*,
Then movies like *The Devil's Rain*.

And then at last the big break came,
The role that really made his name.
He reaped much fame and much reward
When Captain Kirk cried: "All aboard!"

And out among the stars did soar
To Where No Man Had Gone Before.

The *Star Trek* series was a smash
And William Shatner cut a dash
For there was truly no man better
To fill a figure-hugging sweater.

With calming voice and smiling face
He zoomed about in outer space,
And in that inter-stellar trawl
He was the greatest star of all!

Millions of viewers felt they knew
The gallant Captain and his crew:
Doctor McCoy, so skilled and practical
At curing illnesses galactical.

The Captain needed in a crisis
The ship's ingenious devices,
And when a problem got too knotty
"Now beam me up!" he'd order Scotty.

Strangest of all, from Vulcan came
Their colleague, Mr Spock by name,
With ears that pointed at the ceiling.
He was devoid of any feeling
Or passions of the kind that warm us
And yet his brain was quite enormous.

Their starship waged relentless war
On hostile aliens galore.

The Klingons after many chases
Snarled with their corrugated faces
As Kirk confirmed, through storm and strife
The virtues of our way of life.

Now William Shatner, just like Kirk,
Found diets do not always work:
His waist, you'd notice when he's standing,
Is, like the Universe, expanding.

But still the *Star Trek* fans exult –
The fantasy becomes a cult,
And Trekkies meet to shout and cheer
Whenever Kirk or Spock appear.

When William Shatner's on parade
He always gets an accolade.
The greatest compliment is paid
When spoofs and parodies are made.

Web-sites display, without apology,
The First High Church of Shatnerology,
While others tell us, tongue-in-cheek,
The language known as Shatner-Speak.
And William Shatner joins the fun
In shows like *Third Rock from the Sun*.

Though many other shows he'd do –
Films and TV, an album too –
Nothing can ever quite eclipse
The memory of those *Star Trek* trips.

Round William there will always lurk
The sturdy form of Captain Kirk
Who swore throughout the firmament
To boldly go – and boldy went!

GLENN GOULD
(1932 – 1982)

Toronto-born Glenn Gould could play the piano when he was three,
compose at five, and went to the Royal Conservatory of Music when he was ten.
Making his debut at thirteen, he was soon a star of the concert stage,
which he eventually gave up to devote all his time to recording.
His playing style was as individual as his lifestyle, and his recordings
particularly of Bach's keyboard works are admired throughout the world.

For months, while Glenn was in the womb,
His mother in the living-room
Would play the piano every day;
She thought this was the neatest way
To give the child a perfect start
In mastering the pianist's art.

It seems that she was right, for he
Was playing by the age of three.
This infant prodigy, before
He read words, learned to read a score.
Toronto's Royal Conservatory
Gave Glenn, at fourteen, a degree.

And soon Glenn Gould was all the rage,
A star on every concert stage.
The audiences he'd amaze,
Not least with his eccentric ways.

In rumpled clothes he'd sway about
His long wild hair all sticking out.
Conducting gestures too he made
And hummed the music as he played.

And when Glenn Gould began recording
The fans' response was most rewarding.
He'd sleep by day, record at night,
And edit tapes till they were right.
Each phrase was shaped, no note was missed –
Glenn Gould was a perfectionist.

Then suddenly at thirty-one
He shocked and startled everyone:
"I'll play no more on stage!" he said,
"The concert hall will soon be dead!"
Glenn would no longer be on show –
Out of the limelight he would go,
A hermit in his studio.

He did emerge, his tales to tell
In films, and radio shows as well,
Which were as quirky and bizarre
As Glenn's style as a piano star.

His clothes were quite eccentric too:
He'd dress for winter, all year through.
Milkshakes and custard were his diet;
At night his phone was never quiet:
His friends would listen with great patience
To hours of late-night conversations.

The eighty albums Glenn Gould made
Continue to be loved and played.
And yet one day he told a friend:
"I think my funeral at the end
Will not of course attract a throng."

Let's hope he knows now he was wrong:
His fans in hundreds came along.

And Glenn Gould's music found a place
In capsules sent to Outer Space.
So maybe, in a million years
Some alien, exotic ears
Will, on a planet far away
Hear Glenn performing Bach, and say:
"Those Earthlings sure knew how to play!"

NORVAL MORRISSEAU
(born 1932)

*Norval Morrisseau grew up on the Sand Point Reserve in Ontario.
A self-taught artist, he painted the legends of his Ojibwa heritage on
birch-bark and paper. They were seen by an art dealer who brought them
to his gallery in Toronto for an exhibition which made Morrisseau an instant
success, as well as a huge influence in the Canadian art world.*

First Nations were indeed the first
In art and culture to be versed
And long before the whites arrived
Their painting and their carving thrived.

The new arrivals sent those Nations
To go and live on reservations
And there, though poor and most deprived,
Their art and culture still survived.

The Europeans lived apart
And had their own ideas of Art
And so they never got acquainted
With what the native artists painted.

But then Jack Pollock got to know
The work of Norval Morrisseau
In far north-west Ontario.
On birch-bark and on paper too
In strong, bright images he drew
Ojibwa legends which he knew:

Tales of creation, death and birth,
And human struggles here on Earth –
world where spirits can reside
With human beings, side by side.

One thing made his work stand apart,
As Pollock saw, from other art
Which durably and firmly stood
Painted or carved in stone or wood:
These works of Norval Morrisseau
Could be removed and put on show.

And so in 1962
Toronto's art world got to view
A vision startling and new
That came from the Ojibwa Nation
And caused at once a big sensation.

Now overnight the painter came
From poverty to wealth and fame
And Morrisseau was quite surprised
To find himself so lionized.

He'd given Art a fresh dimension
That broke with custom and convention.
Now other Nations' artists too
Adapted Norval's style and view
And Morrisseau had been the start
Of one whole school called Woodland Art –
And now their culture could expect
New understanding and respect.

But Norval Morrisseau would find
Not everyone would be so kind:
At home he'd hear some elders say
Their myths should not be on display.

But Morrisseau went on meanwhile
To shape his individual style
And Expo 67 came
To give his work a world-wide fame.

He'd played his pioneering part
And caused at last the world of Art
To view with new appreciation
The culture of his ancient Nation.

THE DIONNE QUINTS
(born 1934)

The Dionne Quints were the first identical quintuplets to survive.
Their birth in a farmhouse at Callander, Ontario, caused a worldwide sensation,
and brought the family fame and fortune, and many problems too.

The thought of giving birth to Quints
Would make a lot of mothers wince.
When Madame Dionne had her five
No-one believed they could survive.

For they were in a desperate plight:
No water or electric light
Was in the farmhouse where all night
Their mother laboured, giving birth
To this new wonder of the earth.

The doctor and the midwives strove
To warm the Quints before a stove.
A basket there was all they got
To make a cramped and crowded cot.
Their father felt a bit unsteady:
He'd seven children there already.

After a week, the weight they'd reach
Was little more than two pounds each.
And yet Annette and Emilie
Yvonne and Cécile and Marie
Survived to be a famous show
In Callander, Ontario,

And guaranteed the world would know
Of Doctor Allan Roy Dafoe.

For soon a gaggle of reporters
Was swarming round the Dionne daughters.
The newsreels whirred, the flashbulbs popped,
The hectic circus never stopped.
The doctor greeted with felicity
The massive media publicity.

Chicago's World Fair then reacted -
And soon they had Dionne contracted.
Off to the Fair the Quints would go,
Five little stars to steal the show.
But then the Government said "No!"

Ontario's rulers, quick to see
A golden opportunity,
Said, "For the Quints' sake, we declare
We're going to take them into care."

The Quints from home were quickly moved:
The public and the press approved.
They thought it only right - and so
Did Doctor Allan Roy Dafoe.

A hospital was soon erected
Just so the Quints could be protected.
They needed, in the doctor's view,
Protection from their parents too.
In theory they could come to call,
But were not welcomed there at all.

They tried to move in, feeling sore -
But very soon were shown the door.

And yet Dafoe, the Quints' physician,
Said they could go on exhibition.
Inside the hospital was made
A place where they could be displayed.
The children played there in their crèche;
Around the sides, a fine wire mesh
Screened off the eager public, who
Filed slowly past them, peering through.

To see the children, thousands came
To Quintland, as it soon became.
Their dresses must be all the same,
Which led psychologists to claim
Each had no individual role
But looked like guppies in a bowl.

Their guardians ignored such strictures
And put them into motion pictures;
And clearly they were perfect for
Endorsing products by the score.

Milk by Carnation, Oats by Quaker,
Even a disinfectant-maker,
Toothpaste and mattresses and soap
All found a new commercial scope
And soaring sales, upon the basis
Of those five small, cherubic faces.

The locals basked in all this glory:
In books the midwives sold their story.

In Mr Dionne's shop you'd find
Cheap souvenirs of every kind.
He also had a woolen shop,
While the garage where cars would stop
Had five pumps - yes, you get the hint -
Each named after a Dionne Quint.

Their father waged a big campaign
To get the children back again.
It took nine years though, to convince
The world that he should have the Quints.

At last opinion swung his way:
Public and press could now portray
The place made for the Quints to dwell
As very like a prison cell.

The guardians said that there should be
A new house for the family.
The parents then were quite delighted:
They and the Quints were reunited.

But there was little happiness:
Their freedom now was even less.
Their father never let them roam
Outside the fence around their home,
And even kept two bears that growled
At any onlooker who prowled.
Their father, stern and quick to blame,
Still made the Quints all dress the same.

At eighteen they were sent away
To convent school at Nicolet.

Emilie died - her sisters, all
Grief-stricken, moved to Montreal;
And though their parents took it hard
The daughters sent no Christmas card.

Now trust fund arguments were rife
And legal battles dogged their life.
They said then, looking from a distance:
"Money, not love, ruled our existence."

Although such births are now not rare,
There've been no siblings anywhere
So famous, or unlucky, since
Ontario's five Dionne Quints.

JEAN CHRETIEN
(Born 1934)

(Born in Shawinigan, Quebec, Jean Chretien became a lawyer, and his election as a Liberal MP in 1963 was the start of a political career which lasted more than forty years. He led the Liberal Party for thirteen years, ten of them as Prime Minister. His later years were marked by scandal and by feuding with his former colleague Paul Martin, but he retained his public popularity to the end.)

With forty years in politics
Jean Chretien knew all the tricks –
There wasn't much he couldn't fix.

Even when enemies were rife
And Liberals were racked with strife
The battling hero from Shawinigan
Surprised them all by getting in again!

When young, Bell's Palsy made him ill
And left him with paralysis still,
But Jean would make light-hearted quips
About the twisting of his lips:
"Few politicians round the place
Talk with just one side of their face!"

A Trudeau ally from the start,
He always played a major part
In each campaign to keep in check
The Separatists in Quebec.

They called his Clarity Act a shame,
And when the Referendum came

It didn't make their rage diminish
And ended in a photo-finish.

"Where were the Mounties?" people cried
When an intruder got inside
Their house, and Aline with a frown
Wielding a sculpture, faced him down.

The Mounties caused more consternation
Hiring the Disney Corporation.
Their brand-new image brought no luck:
Brickbats the public loved to chuck
And they, like Donald, had to duck!

But Jean did much, with acclamation,
For Canada's image as a nation:
Advanced the cause of Patriation
And set about with style and grit
To grapple with the deficit.
He tackled land-mines, global aid
And North American Free Trade.

Though Clinton was a golfing buddy
The waters after him would muddy
And Chretien firmly told George W. :
"Too bad if our opinions trouble you,
But in Iraq, don't start attacking
Unless you've got the U.N.'s backing."

Although that made George Bush irate,
Jean's standing here at home was great

For showing Canada had clout
When others threw their weight about.

Jean Chretien was just as fiery
Facing the Gomery Inquiry.
Some dubious stories were revealed
Of funds diverted and concealed
And no one was surprised one bit:
Quebec had got the benefit.

With politicians on the spot
It all came down to Who knew What?
Jean said: "No matter what the cost,
The money wasn't really lost.
Besides, whatever happened to it,
It's very clear I didn't do it!"

And then with a magician's grace
He plucked some golf balls from his case.
They didn't scotch a single rumour,
But showed he had a sense of humour.

Jean's overall career was such,
He seemed to have the magic touch.
Though some cried out for his removal
He kept his popular approval.

Paul Martin fumed with rumbling rage
But Chretien stayed centre stage
Until he finally stepped down
And let Paul take the Liberal crown.

So Jean bowed out, with praise and cheers
For all his work of many years,
And not a few shed parting tears.

Now when he saw that his successor
Was deemed by contrast much the lesser,
Did Chretien for a little while
Give just a small, lop-sided smile?

LEONARD COHEN
(born 1934)

Leonard Cohen grew up in an affluent family in Montreal, went to university
at McGill and Columbia, and was one of the group of radical writers
who transformed the Canadian poetry scene. He became a singer
and songwriter and since his first record appeared in 1968 has kept
a large and loyal following of enthusiastic fans in many countries.

Leonard Cohen wrote some poetry
  when he was just a student
And his words they were not tame
  and his words they were not prudent
His classy Westmount background
  he would never let deter him
As an avant-garde protester
  he knew fans would much prefer him.

Soon Leonard started singing
  and he gathered quite a following
In his pool of melancholia
  they were happy to be wallowing
His sombre way of dressing
  couldn't make him look much starker
And his glasses they were dark
  and yet his songs were even darker

And they loved to travel with him
  for they knew that they would find
He had saddened everybody
  with his mind.

His lyrics could be baffling
　　but he never wrote a platitude
Even when he sampled substances
　　designed to change your attitude
He was seeking sacred pathways
　　and he wondered where they ended
But no faith appealed to Leonard
　　even half as much as Zen did.

His forlorn farewells to lovers
　　had a hundred variations
Suzanne and Marianne
　　just had to hear them out with patience
Though the tunes were somewhat similar
　　and the lovers could be scornful
What made the fans delighted
　　was that all of them were mournful

And they loved to travel with him
　　for they knew that they would find
He had saddened everybody
　　with his mind.

DONALD SUTHERLAND
(born 1935)

Donald Sutherland grew up in Bridgewater, Nova Scotia, and went to
the University of Toronto as an engineering student before his acting talents led
him to take up theatre. He moved from stage to film, and a long and versatile
career in over a hundred movies which have made him an international star.

Oh what a credit to his Motherland
Is movie actor Donald Sutherland!
His acting talent was precocious,
This famous son of Nova Scotia's.

Though earlier in his career
He studied as an engineer,
He found the theatre's allure
More dazzling, if much less secure.

He went to England, where he trained
And early stage experience gained;
And then he turned to film instead:
The Castle of the Living Dead
Was Gothic stuff, in horrors rich –
And in it, Donald played a witch.

After more horror movie thrills
He showed his comic acting skills:
The Dirty Dozen was a smash,
Then came his biggest breakthrough, MASH.
As Hawkeye, Sutherland became
A celebrated movie name.

He's acted since without a break:

Five films a year he'd sometimes make.
More than a hundred movies now
Have seen our Donald take a bow
And demonstrated his ability
And quite amazing versatility.

Robbers, detectives, firebugs, spies –
His roles were often a surprise.
The painter Gauguin he portrayed
And Jesus Christ he also played.

He says he is a great respecter
Of all the skills of the director.
"A movie actor's there," he's stated,
"To like to be manipulated."
To back his reverential claims
He gave his kids directors' names.

Donald in recent times has been
Back home upon the theatre scene.
When asked: "Does theatre cause you stress?"
He answered very firmly: "Yes!
Film acting's stressful in its way –
Sometimes you throw up every day!
On stage you're stressed when you appear –
It's just a different kind of fear.
But both have got as compensation
Their own immense exhilaration."

So Donald Sutherland continues
To flex his strong artistic sinews,
Enhancing with his gleaming radiance
The galaxy of star Canadians!

PAUL MARTIN
(Born 1938)

(Paul Martin was born in Windsor, Ontario, and his career in law and business included the ownership of Canada Steamship Lines. Like his father, he became a leading figure in the Liberal Party, and as Finance Minister succeeded in erasing a multi-billion dollar deficit and bringing in five budget surpluses in a row. His rivalry with Prime Minister Jean Chretien became more and more bitter, and when Chretien stepped down he was elected leader. His three years at the top were marked by indecision and scandal, and eventual electoral defeat.)

Paul came from true Liberal stock
A chip of the old family block,
But commercially too
His expertise grew
And his ships floated high in the dock.

Like his father, young Paul set his sights
On gaining the Liberal heights
But Jean Chretien's clout
Saw Paul Martin knocked out
In the first of their rancorous fights.

Yet Chretien gave him the chance
When he put him in charge of finance,
And Paul didn't fudge it
He balanced the Budget
And the nation went on to advance.

For years, though the surpluses grew,
Paul was feeling increasingly blue
He champed at the bit

For he felt he was fit
To captain the Liberal crew.

The feud grew increasingly bitter
Each man was a real heavy hitter.
Jean gave him the sack
But Paul Martin came back –
He simply would not be a quitter.

So at last, after Jean's resignation,
Paul was chosen, to Liberal elation
With rock stars and all
They were having a ball
At what looked like a canonization.

Alas, his charisma would wither
And party got the slithers.
It might be a pity
To rule by committee
For soon he was called Mister Dithers.

He found it a problem to handle
The Liberals' flickering candle
And how they all reeled
At what was revealed
By reports of the sponsorship scandal.

For Paul, it's the saddest of stories:
He was part of the party's great glories
But he ended the trip
When the Liberal ship
Was finally sunk by the Tories!

BRIAN MULRONEY
(Born 1939)

*(Born in Baie-Comeau, Quebec, where his Irish immigrant father worked
as an electrician in the paper mill, Brian Mulroney got involved with
Conservative politics as a student at St. Francis Xavier University in
Nova Scotia. He returned to Quebec to take a law degree at Laval, and to become
a key figure in the party. He went on to lead the Progressive Conservatives
to their record-breaking victory in 1984)*

He was an electrician's son –
Mulroney was his name.
He wanted to be Number One
And stake his claim to fame.

For power and prestige he yearned
And at St. Francis Xavier
With glad hands and with smiles he learned
Political behaviour.

He courted all of the elite
Whose praise he hoped to win
And everywhere, they seemed to meet
That formidable chin.

That long profile was also high:
He flourished at the Bar;
The Cliche Commission by and by
Made Brian a rising star.

He'd never deigned to try the test
Of ordinary election –

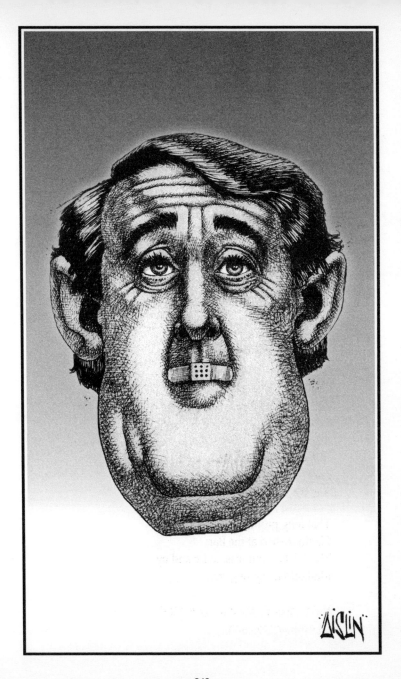

Yet he decided he'd contest
The leadership selection.

Some thought it brave, some thought it brash,
But Brian went on with patience
And with the help of lots of cash
From corporate donations.

He failed, but later on that quest
Once more he would embark.
This time his colleagues were impressed:
Mulroney beat Joe Clark.

Just one year later Brian was proud
To claim his finest hour.
Big Business cheered long and loud:
The Tories were in power!

With tycoons Brian was in cahoots,
The businessman's Prime Minister.
It wasn't just his taste in suits
That Liberals found sinister.

The nation he would soon divide
As Liberal tempers frayed
When resolutely Brian tried
To introduce Free Trade.

He sang with Reagan and with Bush
To get towards his goals,
And then he made the final push
And triumphed at the polls.

Another goal he tried to reach
Was sorting out Quebec;
He sailed upon the Lake of Meech
But found a slippery deck.

Not all of the provincial crew
Agreed to stay on board.
Said Brian: "Instead I'll bring to you
The Charlottetown Accord!"

A referendum then said No;
Quebec toyed with secession.
Brian's popularity was low
Because of the recession.

And what with that, and GST,
His status on the slide,
Mulroney said: "It's time for me
Perhaps to step aside."

Kim Campbell was the one he'd tip –
Was there a hint of malice?
She found the Tory leadership
To be a poisoned chalice.

Tories hailed Brian as P.M.
In 1984;
His leadership had given them
Two hundred seats and more.

But now in 1993
Conservatives were mad:

The outcome was calamity –
Two seats were all they had!

With Brian, the party's rise and fall
Had both been meteoric,
But he was certain, most of all,
His reign had been historic.

He said: "The Liberals' secret is
Quite easy to divine:
They've just adopted policies
Identical to mine!"

JONI MITCHELL
(born 1943)

*Joni Mitchell grew up in Saskatoon where she first performed in coffee houses.
Later in Toronto and then in Los Angeles her individual style and original songs
made her a star on the performance circuit and on records.*

Joni was born in Fort MacLeod
And made her parents very proud.
She later said they'd counted on
A boy they'd christen Robert John,
But when the baby's sex was known
They changed it to Roberta Joan.

Some frugal times the family knew
In prairie towns where Joni grew.
She suffered a near-fatal blow
At nine years old, from polio;
But struggling bravely, she survived
And as a lithe teenager thrived.

She loved the party dancing scene,
Won contests as a Teenage Queen
And listened to rock music daily -
Then bought herself a ukulele.

Though modern styles did not come soon
To prairie towns like Saskatoon
Its coffee house, Louis Riel,
Was where the trendier types did well.

Tonite!
JONI
MITCHELL

Sorry! Parking lot is full

Glenvale
Auditorium

There Joni started her career;
Most liked her, although some would sneer.
At least she earned enough reward
To mean that now she could afford
 A real guitar, which all were thinking
Outclassed the ukulele's plinking.

And with this brand-new instrument
She started to experiment.
Eccentric tuning styles she made
To match whatever song she played,
And found her voice could quickly change
To span a most impressive range.

That range made Joni quite unique:
Like birds that glide from peak to peak
Ruling their kingdom in the sky
Her voice swooped low or soared up high.

"She sounds," one critic chose to grouse,
"Like someone swallowing a mouse!"
But many others found her voice
As classy as the best Rolls Royce.

Her toothy smile, her long blonde hair,
Made her distinctive everywhere.
In 1967 came
Her Chart success, The Circle Game.
Then with her reputation growing
She found she had the Urge for Going.

From town to town she made her way:
Toronto, New York, then L.A.
In Laurel Canyon there she stayed
And wrote the moving songs she played
And found she had a fortune made:
For writing songs and then recording
Had proved for Joni most rewarding.

She formed a lucrative creation,
Her own big music corporation;
And just to make the fortune swell
She purchased real estate as well.
She said, "I'm now, by some strange twist,
The only hippie capitalist!"
Relationships were less secure,
And restless Joni used to tour -
Guitar-case crammed with routes and maps
And lyrics scrawled on paper scraps.

Star rock groups Joni moved among
Like Crosby, Stills and Nash and Young -
Found love and lost it, went abroad
Where thousands gathered to applaud,
Spent time in Crete where hippie raves
Were held among the mountain caves.

But not all Joni's ways were wild -
Her life was often calm and mild:
She liked to cook and paint and knit,
Play cribbage when she'd time for it.

While as for fame, it waxed and waned.

Sometimes as Queen of Rock she reigned,
Her records reaching such success
Elvis himself was selling less.
Though sometimes too we must confess
She languished in the wilderness.

Now, Joni Mitchell's here to stay -
Grammy Awards have come her way
And most of all, her fans in throngs
Remember Joni's subtle songs:

Her poetry of love that ends,
Of hope and freedom, fickle friends,
Dreams of a river to skate away on,
Of Chelsea Mornings to greet the day on,
Of the paradise we haven't got,
Now paved to make a parking lot.
As one enamoured critic found:
"If angels sang, that's how they'd sound!"

252

GILLES VILLENEUVE
(1950-1982)

*Born in Quebec, Gilles Villeneuve was a champion snowmobile racer before
he took up motor-racing. His daredevil style on the Formula Atlantic
and Formula One circuits, as well as his personal charm, made him a hugely
popular figure in Canada and abroad. He was killed in a collision at
the age of 32, but his name lives on in Montreal's Grand Prix Circuit
and in the motor-racing triumphs of his son Jacques.*

No racer was faster than Gilles
He had such magnetic appeal
   He first took the lead
   At phenomenal speed
When he raced in his sleek snowmobile
   VROOM, VROOM!

When he went into Formula Atlantic
His prowess was truly gigantic
   In one year, he'd first places
   In nine major races
And the fans' jubilation was frantic!
   VROOM, VROOM!

In flying, snowmobiling or driving
He was mostly the first one arriving
   The risks that he'd take
   Would make other men quake
For on danger he felt he was thriving!
   VROOM, VROOM!

And when to Ferrari he'd gone
His star in Grand Prix races shone
    His career was cut short
    In this perilous sport
But Villeneuve's name will live on -
    VROOM, VROOM!

DAN AYKROYD
(Born 1952)

(Dan Aykroyd was born in Ottawa, and studied Criminology at Carleton University before deciding on an acting career. He began on stage with the Second City *company, moved to television as a star of* Saturday Night Live,*then on to a movie career as actor and writer on more than fifty films.)*

At Carleton, studying things criminal,
Dan found the laughter content minimal –
And so he thought he'd make a shift
To exercise his comic gift.

He joined Toronto's *Second City*
In shows satirical and witty.
Delighted audiences flocked
To see the proud and pompous mocked.
(Some thought the group's name was the worst:
Surely Toronto should be First?!)

And then came television fame:
Saturday Night Live made his name.
A founder member of the cast,
Dan now, though thirty years have passed,
Still pops up there with regularity
In scenes of humour and hilarity.
And then, perhaps what pleased him most,
He finally became its host.

With John Belushi as a friend
On and off screen, good times he'd spend.
Blues Brothers, with its car-chase stunts

Caused the producers more than once
To wince at costs – Dan could exult:
The movie has become a cult.

And there were further hectic chases
With Eddie Murphy, *Trading Places*.
Driving Miss Daisy also came
To bring its actors great acclaim.
For Dan, as well as acclamation,
It brought an Oscar nomination.

In many movies, he's appeared
With creatures creepy, crazed and weird.
In *Ghostbusters*, as Doctor Stantz,
The monsters never stood a chance.
The *Alien Stepmother* was hell
And *Coneheads* cast an ugly spell.

Some films Dan Aykroyd wrote as well:
The cops who often feature there
Reflect an interest he can share:
He sometimes offers for inspection
His cherished police-force badge collection.

He goes in squad cars with the force
And rides a policeman's bike, of course.
And he can boast an added bounty:
A grandfather who was a Mountie.

His forebears also liked to nurture
A role as psychical researcher.
Dan made this fascination formal:
His series on the paranormal

Rock on!
Dan Aykroyd
aka Elwood
aka Beldar
aka Doctor
Stantz
etc...

Showed off a new side of the actor –
They called the television show *Psi Factor*.

Dan Aykroyd there has been the host
To many a tale of ghoul and ghost,
Poltergeist probes and eerie jaunts
To spooky supernatural haunts.
Viewers were always entertained
By stories of the Unexplained.

No mystery shrouds Dan's success –
His talent got him there, no less.
To us he need make no apology
That he abandoned Criminology.

BRET "HITMAN" HART
(born 1957)

Bret Hart grew up in Calgary in a family of wrestlers: his father Stu ran the celebrated Stampede Circuit for many years. He has won the World Heavyweight Championship title six times, and was a key figure in the battles for control between the two big wrestling federations, as well as appearing in film documentaries and TV drama series.

The champion, Bret "Hitman" Hart,
Always looked like a star from the start.
With his hold, the Sharpshooter,
His rivals he'd neuter
And tear them all slowly apart.

Bret's father the wrestler would say:
"Our cellar's ideal for the fray."
He had his boys plungin'
Down into 'The Dungeon'
To practise for five hours a day.

When Bret as a pro was appearing
His boyish good looks were endearing;
Though his hair in the headlocks
Was like stringy dreadlocks
His charm had the fans up and cheering.

His athletic and muscular bulk
Could cause other wrestlers to sulk.
In his dashing pink tights
He won legions of fights
With guys like King Kong, Snake, and Hulk.

Every wrestler must have the appeal
Of a good "Babyface" or bad "Heel".
Though their falls, like a dance,
 Are all planned in advance,
The blood that they shed is for real!

Bret's wrestling career was to bring
Many fights, in and out of the ring –
But his fame it still grows
And all Calgary knows
That their local boy is the King!

TERRY FOX
(1958 – 1981)

(Born in Winnipeg and brought up in Port Coquitlam, BC,
Terry Fox was only eighteen when his right leg had to be amputated
because of bone cancer. Watching the suffering of his fellow cancer patients,
he determined to raise funds for research to help conquer the disease.
So began his Marathon of Hope, which continues to be run annually
in his honour and has raised over $300 million dollars worldwide)

School friends might have said of Terry
Basketball was not his scene.
In a team of nineteen players
He was rated just Nineteen.

Yet he aimed for sporting prowess
And a brilliant career;
And when Terry graduated
He was Athlete of the Year.

That career was cruelly shortened –
With the operation done
And his right leg amputated
How could Terry hope to run?

Terry Fox would not be beaten
And he planned a daunting test:
He would run across the country,
Every mile from east to west.

After months of painful training,
Sponsors wondered, could he cope?

In St. John's, they watched him starting
On his Marathon of Hope.

Terry, standing by the harbour,
Dipped his new leg in the tide.
To another distant ocean
He was sure he'd make it stride.

With his boyhood friend Doug Alward
There behind him in the van
Terry Fox's epic journey
Over Newfoundland began.

Newfoundland, then Nova Scotia
And Prince Edward Island too –
Everywhere the crowds would gather,
Urge him on and cheer him through.

In the dark, before the sunrise,
Every day they woke at four.
Every day saw Terry running
Twenty gruelling miles and more.

Those who came to watch him running
With his clumping step-and-hop,
Wondered how he kept on going
On and on without a stop.

Running with his legs uncovered
Even in the freezing rain,
Even when his leg-stump, bleeding,
Made him clench his fists in pain.

The Marathon of Hope went onward
And although it gave him fame,
Raising funds for treating cancer,
That was Terry's only aim.

As he passed them, there were people
Pressing dollars in his hand.
There were gifts, and cash collected
From each corner of the land.

Through Quebec and through Ontario,
Through the storms and heat he passed.
Then near Thunder Bay, he wondered
If this mile would be his last.

Doctors found the cancer spreading –
Terry now could hardly stand.
There could be no happy ending
For the marathon he planned.

Many thousands wept in mourning
When they learned that he was gone.
Terry Fox's fight had ended –
But his Marathon goes on.

STEPHEN HARPER
(Born 1959)

*(Stephen Harper was first elected as a Reform Party MP for Calgary West
in 1993, and later led the Canadian Alliance in Opposition.
In 2003 he co-founded the Conservative Party of Canada, which he led
to victory in the federal election of 2006)*

Jean Chretien used to play trombone
And now a Harper takes the throne.
We yearned to know what tunes he brings
And most of all, who pulls the strings?

A motley band must help him rock:
The NDP now, and the Bloc.
Dependence on those varied votes
Could cause a few discordant notes.

He is a Beatles devotee:
Perhaps he plans to Let It Be.
Though Love Me Do is his delight
Could Harper face A Hard Day's Night?

WAYNE GRETZKY
(born 1961)

*When still in his teens, Wayne Gretzky began his spectacular career with
the Edmonton Oilers, helping them to win four Stanley Cups in five years.
He later joined the Los Angeles Kings and the St Louis Blues.
He broke over sixty NHL records and went on to be honoured as
the best hockey player of all time – "The Great One".*

A jersey labelled 99
Was lifted up on high
To shouts and cheers and many tears
When Gretzky said goodbye.

The man they call The Great One –
A name he truly earned –
Always so proud to please the crowd,
To Edmonton returned.

For here his greatest triumphs
Those cheering crowds inspired.
It was a blow for them to know
That Gretzky had retired.

This skinny kid from Brantford
Fulfilled his boyhood dream
And made his name and gained his fame
Upon the Oilers' team.

The hockey records tumbled
The scores they mounted up.
The sparkling goals arrived in shoals
So did the Stanley Cup.

269

He scored more goals than anyone
In all the NHL.
He never missed with his assists –
Oh how those records fell!

The day that Wayne and Janet
Up to the altar went,
The grand parades and accolades
Were like a royal event.

Wayne Gretzky's sporting image
Was always squeaky clean,
So he got lots of TV spots
For products on the screen.

He also played for Canada
With passion and with pride:
The Maple Leaf in his belief
Adorned the greatest side.

And in the States, the President
Would even bow before him:
He was so famed that Reagan claimed
He'd swap all Texas for him!

"Just one more year!" the fans all cried,
"You're greatest of the Greats!"
Wayne said: "The Hall of Fame has all
My hockey sticks and skates!"

"So farewell to you, hockey fans,
For I must leave you now."
The rafters shook as Gretzky took
His last and final bow.

JULIE PAYETTE
(Born 1963)

(Julie Payette was born in Montreal and studied engineering and computer science at McGill and Toronto universities. In 1992 she was selected for astronaut training by the Canadian Space Agency. She joined the crew of the space shuttle Discovery *which travelled to the International Space Station in 1999.)*

When Julie was young you can bet
Her sights on high flying were set.
As a child she would follow
The flights of Apollo
Saying: "I'll be an astronaut yet!"

The attraction of space was hypnotic
Her research refined and exotic
On machines you can teach
To recognize speech
And arms whose controls are robotic.

She believes you should have versatility –
She runs, skis and swims with agility;
Her piano inspires
And she sings with top choirs
And has wide multilingual ability.

When Canada's space-planners met
New astronaut trainees to vet,
Of five thousand and more
They selected just four
And among them was Julie Payette.

SHANIA TWAIN
(Born 1965)

*(Shania Twain grew up in poor circumstances in
Timmins, Ontario, and even as a child she sang in clubs and bars.
She continued in the music business and hit the real big time when she met and
married record producer Mutt Lange. She is now the biggest selling female solo
artist in the world, packing in the crowds at huge stadiums everywhere.)*

From Timbuctoo to Tallahassee
Fans in millions hold her dear:
The lassie with the sassy chassis,
Bubbling with relentless cheer.

You'd have to be a Jeremiah
Not to warm to sweet Shania.

Her mother scorned the warning not to
Put your daughter on the stage,
Told Shania she had got to
Go out there and earn a wage.

Clubs and bars became her scene
Long before she turned thirteen.

Nashville then had all the action –
She sang country for a while;
Then she fell for Mutt's attraction –
Rock and roll was more his style.

Mutt's talents quite belied his name
And took them both to wealth and fame.

Songs both glad and melancholic
She and Mutt spend months creating.
A life some say is workaholic
They would call exhilarating.

And she has no cause to wonder:
"Whose bed have your boots been under?"

Once she went for tomboy dressing –
Now it's often silver boots,
Hotpants, veils her form caressing,
Leopard-spotted trouser suits.

Critics call her act robotic
And mechanically erotic.

Critics – fans would like to flatten 'em,
Forever and For Always loyal.
Albums all go multi-platinum
And they treat her like a royal.

Nothing her career can scupper –
She's *UP, UP, UP,* and going UPPER!

CELINE DION
(born 1968)

*Celine Dion grew up in Charlemagne, Quebec, in a musical family,
and composed her first song at the age of twelve. She went on to become
a world-famous singing star, selling millions of records and winning Oscars
for movie theme songs, as well as a host of other awards.*

"My heart," declared Celine Dion,
"Will certainly go on and on,
And on and on and on and on,
Just like the endless song I sang
The night the ship's alarm bells rang
And everyone began to panic
Aboard the stately, doomed Titanic.
My voice of course remained to float
Upon the waves – unlike the boat."

This future star pop-music queen
Was born the youngest of fourteen.
At five, the tuneful tot would be
Performing with the family –
An infant prodigy was she.

When she was twelve, Celine Dion
Composed her very first chanson.
For René Angelil, the demo
Caused him to say: "Now, take a memo!
This little girl is going far –
I plan on making her a star.
And to be sure her records sell,
I'll be her manager as well."

So in her teens the young Celine
Was launched upon the music scene.
She very quickly reached the top
And then she never seemed to stop.

Most of the songs Celine recorded
With praise and prizes were rewarded.
Some envious glances she might get
From Shania Twain and Morrissette
But as for rivals, she could flatten 'em
With countless discs of gold and platinum.

Albums like Falling into You
Meant her success just grew and grew.
An Oscar came when she released
The theme for Beauty and the Beast.

Let's Talk About Love was one big title –
And to her, love was always vital.
It featured in most everything
Celine composed or chose to sing.

Some critics, looking for her faults,
Said she was wallowing in schmaltz;
One even dared compare her sound
To being in maple syrup drowned.

Love ruled her music, and her life,
For she became her guru's wife:
René she wed, once and for all,
At Notre Dame, in Montreal.

Not once and for all, as things turned out:
In case there should be any doubt,
Just five years later they'd decide
To act again as groom and bride.
A farewell concert she would do
(The latest one of quite a few)
Then to Las Vegas they were heading
To stage a most flamboyant wedding.

A ballroom was, for this event,
Transformed into a Bedouin tent.
Celine's dress looked like gold enamel
And dazzled every watching camel.

Jugglers performed, musicians played,
A belly-dancer writhed and swayed.
The pair on chairs were carried in
And then the wedding could begin.
They both held candles, then drank up
In turn, wine from a golden cup.

The ritual wasn't over yet:
They each put on a coronet,
And all this weird, elaborate show
Took up twelve pages in "Hello!"

Now some, bored by the goings-on
Of René and Celine Dion
Might only hope, with many a sigh,
This time, "Hello!" might mean: "Goodbye!"
Though others think that outlook's noir
And would prefer an "Au Revoir!"

SASQUATCH

*The Sasquatch, also known as Bigfoot, is a tall hairy creature believed
to inhabit the mountains and forests of the Canadian and American northwest.
Many sightings have been reported and many footprints found,
but scientists are still not certain whether the Sasquatch and its similar
Himalayan counterpart, the Yeti, are mythical or real.*

The Sasquatch, so the story goes,
Has long arms, and a wide, flat nose.
He walks tall — there's no doubt of that —
He's nine feet high, without a hat.

Though tales of his appearance vary,
They all agree he's very hairy.
His four-foot chest is like a wall,
He seems to have no neck at all:
In fact, his build would make him seem
A natural for the football team.

His big toe's huge, his feet the same;
No wonder, when he rose to fame,
That BIGFOOT was his other name.

In folklore, though it's hardly science,
He is descended from the Giants
Who fought in two ferocious bands
Among the northwest forest lands.
Their gentler offspring, legends say,
Roam in those mountain woods today.

Some claim he's cousin to the Yeti
Whose footprints, scattered like confetti,
Make disbelief seem simply petty.
But skeptics still maintain that no men
Have seen Abominable Snowmen.

The Bigfoot Sasquatch, though, has been
By many different people seen.
Even a film for one whole minute
Has claimed to have the creature in it.
This claim some scientists refute
And say the figure, though hirsute,
Is someone in a monkey suit.

Earlier, miners in a shack
Claimed they'd been subject to attack.
When skeptics said, once more aloof:
"If that's a Sasquatch, where's the proof?"
The miners growled: "Then who, you goof,
Spent all night pounding on the roof?"

One Albert Ostman claimed that he
At Toba Inlet, in B.C.,
Was kidnapped by a family.
One night when he was camping out
A giant Sasquatch lurked about,
And gathered up his gear, then crept
And picked up Ostman as he slept.

He took him home to meet the wife,
And Ostman shared their Sasquatch life.
Their son and daughter too were there:

The captive was a sight so rare
They never ceased to laugh and stare.

Although they offered him no harm,
He found the life had little charm.
He slipped away into the distance —
At least he'd proof of their existence!
The only proof, though, was his word,
And few believed in what they heard.

In spite of countless sightings more
And sets of prints of feet galore
The skeptics say that these alone
Are not enough, just on their own.
They say that not one hair or bone
Or even tooth has once been shown.

So where have all the Sasquatch gone?
The controversy rages on.
Are Yetis, Bigfoots, and Sasquatches
Seen only after several scotches?

Are they as fictional as Chaucer,
Or creatures from a Flying Saucer?
And more believable or less
Than Monsters living in Loch Ness?

Perhaps they're prudently deciding
It's safer if they stay in hiding.
Who wants to be coralled in zoos,
Or pictured on the TV News?

Perhaps the truth we'll never know.
There's one big question lurking, though:
However we may fret and fuss,
Do Sasquatches believe in us?

AUTHOR'S NOTE

In the ten years since Aislin and I got together to produce the first of our series of Canadian characters, I have been exhilarated and impressed by the amazing variety of personalities Canada has produced: explorers, statesmen, writers and artists, performers, eccentrics, sporting stars, inventors, spies, bootleggers, and charming chancers - as well as such exotic creatures as the Canada Goose, Sasquatch and Winnie the Pooh.

It has been a great delight to pay a sincere and humorous tribute to them in my verses, and to see Aislin's briliant artistic creations alongside them.

I want to thank the Canadian Embassy in Dublin and the London Library for their help with my research, as well as Marsha Boulton for her series of *JUST A MINUTE* biographies.

Above all, my thanks go to Aislin for his hilarious and incisive illustrations, to Mary Hughson for her elegant design and production, and to our great editor and publisher, Kim McArthur.

Gordon Snell

CARTOONIST'S NOTE

My talented colleague, Gordon Snell, has expressed his thanks to just about everyone involved with this book. Therefore, there is no one left to thank but him!

Terry Mosher (Aislin)